CRITICAL PEDAGOGY AND SOCIAL CHANGE

This powerful and accessible text breaks with tradition by teasing out mere assumptions, and provides a concrete illustration and critique of today's critical pedagogy. Veteran teacher educator Seehwa Cho begins the book with an engaging overview of the history of critical pedagogy and a clear, concise breakdown of key concepts and terms. Not content to hide behind rhetoric, Cho forces herself and the reader to question the most basic assumptions of critical pedagogy, such as what a vision of social change really means. After a thoughtful and pithy analysis of the politics, possibilities, and agendas of mainstream critical pedagogy, Cho takes the provocative step of arguing that these dominant discourses are ultimately what stifle the possibility for true social change. Without focusing on micro-level approaches to alternatives, Cho concludes by laying out some basic principles and future directions for critical pedagogy.

Both accessible and provocative, *Critical Pedagogy and Social Change* is a significant contribution to the debates over critical pedagogy and a fresh, much-needed examination of teaching and learning for social justice in the classroom and community beyond.

Seehwa Cho is Associate Professor of Teacher Education, University of St. Thomas in Minnesota, USA.

The Critical Social Thought Series
Edited by Michael W. Apple,
University of Wisconsin–Madison

CRITICAL PEDAGOGY AND SOCIAL CHANGE

Critical Analysis on the Language of Possibility

Seehwa Cho

Routledge
Taylor & Francis Group

NEW YORK AND LONDON

First published 2013
by Routledge
711 Third Avenue, New York, NY 10017

Simultaneously published in the UK
by Routledge
2 Park Square, Milton Park, Abingdon, Oxon OX14 4RN

Routledge is an imprint of the Taylor & Francis Group, an informa business

Library of Congress Cataloging in Publication Data
Cho, Seehwa.
   Critical pedagogy and social change: critical analysis on the
   language of possibility/Seehwa Cho.
   pages cm.—(The critical social thought series)
   Includes bibliographical references and index.
   1. Critical pedagogy. 2. Social justice. I. Title.
   LC196.C46 2012
   370.11′5—dc23   2012010544

ISBN: 978-0-415-88610-9 (hbk)
ISBN: 978-0-415-88611-6 (pbk)
ISBN: 978-0-203-82921-9 (ebk)

Typeset in Minion and Scala Sans
by Florence Production Ltd, Stoodleigh, Devon, UK

Printed and bound in the United States of America
by Edwards Brothers, Inc.

To my parents and my daughter

CONTENTS

SERIES EDITOR'S INTRODUCTION

Most nations—and nations to be—have a history of people asking critical questions about schooling. Does schooling simply reproduce the ideological goals and cultural forms and content of dominant groups? Could schooling be used to raise serious issues about existing societies? Could it go even further and be reorganized so that it actively participated in the reconstruction of those societies?

In the United States, the figure who was most notable for raising these questions was George S. Counts. He is seen as one of the key—if not the key—figures in challenging educators to press forward with an agenda of social transformation. His small book, *Dare the School Build a New Social Order?* (Counts 1932), stands as a classic statement of the demand that educators commit themselves and the institutions in which they work to a clear goal of challenging major capitalist assumptions and processes. Internationally, Paulo Freire deservedly stands as one of the most significant figures, both asking these questions and providing tools for engaging in the process of actually doing the social, cultural, and educational work necessary for such transformation to go on. Within minoritized communities, W.E.B.

Du Bois, Carter G. Woodson, and C.L.R. James have provided powerful analyses and resources for this process as well. Many other names of course could be noted.

The fact that there is a long history of engaging with these questions and providing critical answers to them—and, just as importantly, providing substantive ways of doing critical education—should remind us of the range of material that deserves the name "critical." In *The Routledge Handbook of Critical Education*, Wayne Au, Luis Armando Gandin, and I point to the emerging multiplicity of theories, politics, and practices that are seen to be part of critical education (Apple, Au, & Gandin 2009). These tendencies include arguments based in Marxist and neo-Marxist approaches, in poststructural and postmodern analyses, in critical race theory, in feminisms, in indigenous struggles and epistemologies, in disability movements, in queer theory, and the list could and does go on. All of them have their roots in a profound dissatisfaction with dominant economic, social, and cultural relations and with the forms of education that are generated out of and reproduce these relations. Many of them as well go beyond the act of "bearing witness to negativity" and go further into the process of building alternatives to these forms of education (Apple, 2010; in press).

Many of those within the critical education communities (the plural is important here) self-consciously see themselves as participating in building on the tradition of "critical pedagogy." The roots of this are varied and the names associated with it are equally varied. But understanding these roots is crucial, since like all fields there is the danger of a loss of collective memory about why such radical questions were asked, of the theoretical and political groundings of these questions, and of what institutions they were asked about.

Seehwa Cho critically analyzes the strengths and weaknesses of a good deal of the literature in and arguments of critical pedagogy. What sets *Critical Pedagogy and Social Change* apart from other works is the kind of powerful questions it asks of the critical pedagogy and critical theory traditions in education. Cho asks whether these positions, as they have been taken up in education, have become less powerful than they should be. In essence, she asks whether they are radical enough to deal with the kinds of economic, political, and ideological relations that dominate societies like our own. Her answer is one that may trouble some people within the critical pedagogy community(ies). In essence, she claims that much of what goes by the name of critical pedagogy has become rhetorical and has cut itself off from a robust understanding of the complex nature of the structures of exploitation and domination and the relations that underpin them.

This is "sisterly" criticism, since Cho herself is deeply committed to critical projects, both intellectually and politically, in education and the larger society. And even if some of the readers of this book may disagree with parts of her arguments, we would all do well to take seriously the fundamental issues she raises and the criticisms she makes. In the process, Cho asks important questions that need to be answered by the many people who have rightly been influenced by the traditions within critical pedagogy.

It has become something of a truism in the literature in analytic philosophy that language does and can do many things, all of them valuable. It can be used to describe, explain, control, critique, legitimate, affiliate, and mobilize (Austin 1962; see also Wittgenstein 1963). Rhetorical language is associated with legitimation, affiliation, and mobilization; but it is often a poor tool for the other tasks that language must perform. This is an important point that bears on the arguments made in *Critical Pedagogy and Social Change*. Parts of the critical pedagogy tradition seem to be content with critical slogans, rather than examining the complicated and multiple structures and power relations that exist in the real world and the full range of possible tactics that might be employed to change them.

This is a pity since this lack has a number of negative effects. It weakens the explanatory potential of critical analyses. It helps those who wish to marginalize such analyses at exactly the time at which they are of most importance. And finally, such rhetorical positions lack the strategic sensibility that is so crucial in what Antonio Gramsci calls a "war of position," a nuanced understanding of the actual possibilities of doing critical work in multiple sites (see, e.g., Gramsci, 1971).

This is not true of all of the critical traditions of course. Some of the most interesting work in critical pedagogy is much less rhetorical and is grounded in the concrete understanding of and action in communities and social movements and with cultural activists and practicing educators at all levels of the educational system (see, e.g., Watson, 2010; Apple, 2010; Apple, Au, & Gandin, 2009). This kind of work would no doubt find approval from Cho. I am certain as well that she would approve of much of the more robust and nuanced theoretical and political analyses that have emerged on the state, on the complex relationships among culture, politics, and the economy, and on the ways in which educational sites and institutions can be worked on and with that have been developed during the past decades of intense conceptual and political progress (see, e.g., Lipman, 2011; Wright, 2010; Apple, 2006; Apple, 2012).

Critical Pedagogy and Social Change points to a number of these developments, at the same time as it reminds us to reconnect with the social visions and critical impulses that can serve as the fundament of our critical work inside and outside of education. It may be a relatively short book, but its implications are large. Once you read it, you will see what I mean.

Michael W. Apple
John Bascom Professor of Curriculum and Instruction
and Educational Policy Studies,
University of Wisconsin, Madison

References

Apple, M.W. (2006). *Educating the "right" way: Markets, standards, god, and inequality*, 2nd edition. New York: Routledge.

Apple, M.W. (Ed.) (2010). *Global crises, social justice, and education*. New York: Routledge.

Apple, M.W. (2012). *Education and power*, Routledge Classic Edition. New York: Routledge.

Apple, M.W. (in press). *Can education change society?* New York: Routledge.

Apple, M.W., Au, W., and Gandin, L. A. (Eds.) (2009). *The Routledge international handbook of critical education*. New York: Routledge.

Austin, J.L. (1962). *How to do things with words*. Cambridge, MA: Harvard University Press.

Counts, G.S. (1932). *Dare the school build a new social order?* New York: John Day.

Gramsci, A. (1971). *Selections from the Prison Notebooks*. New York: International Publishers.

Lipman, P. (2011). *The new political economy of urban education*. New York: Routledge.

Watson, V. (2012). *Learning to liberate*. New York: Routledge.

Wittgenstein, L. (1963). *Philosophical investigations*. Oxford: Blackwell.

Wright, E.O. (2010). *Envisioning real utopias*. New York: Routledge.

ACKNOWLEDGMENTS

I am fortunate to have (and have had) two great mentors, without whom this book would not have been possible. First, I am thankful to Michael Apple, who guided me academically during my fledgling years at the University of Wisconsin. It was a pleasure to have an advisor with a great mind, and a warm heart. I do not remember all the courses I took at the time, but I still remember (and always will) how much I learned and enjoyed the famous "Friday Seminar." My appreciation and gratitude for Michael's teaching and guidance has only deepened with time, as I now aspire to be the mentor he was to me to my own students. Second, Tullio Maranhão was a colleague, a friend, and above all, my mentor in life. Until his passing, we shared many conversations over meals and wine. While our time together was cut short, I am grateful to my dear friend for pushing me to expand and grow both intellectually and academically. If he were alive today, Tullio would have been proud to see this book, finally, go to print.

Special thanks goes to my dear friend, Zeus Leonardo, for encouraging me to write this book. For years, he has been my intellectual partner. I remember, with fondness, many conversations and sometimes heated debates we have had over many lunches. It is a great pleasure to have a friend with such a brilliant mind. I also have to thank the many doctoral students I have taught in critical pedagogy and education leadership programs. I have learned much from them. There are many other friends and individuals who have taught me a lot over the years. Among them are John Seipp, Yeanju Lee, Kerry Frank, Jan Frank, Candace Chou, Stephen Phillion, Pat Burdell, Sheena Choi, Young-ok An, and Heekyung Kang Youn.

I would like to express my gratitude to the University of St. Thomas, for providing me time to write this book by granting sabbatical leave and a research grant. Much appreciation goes to my editor at Routledge, Catherine Bernard, for enduring several delays on my part and for providing insightful suggestions. And finally, and most importantly, there are not enough words to express my thanks to my daughter, Seorim. She has had to comb through this book, and has had to fix all my tangled sentences. But above all, I know without her support, this book would not have seen the light. I am glad that she knows how special she is to me.

PERMISSIONS

Cho, S. (2006). On language of possibility: Revisiting critical pedagogy. In C. Rossatto, R. Allen, & M. Pruyn (Eds.), *Reinventing critical pedagogy: Widening the circle of anti-oppression education.* Lanham, MD: Rowman & Littlefield.

Cho, S. (2010). Politics of critical pedagogy and new social movements, *Educational Philosophy and Theory*, 42(3): 310–325.

Cho, S. (2010). Why Culture? The political economy of cultural politics. In Z. Leonardo (Ed.), *Handbook of cultural politics and education.* Rotterdam: Sense Publishers.

1

INTRODUCTION

The Questions and Goals of the Book

Critical pedagogy emerged in the 1980s as a relatively new field within critical education, claiming to find a "language of possibility" (Giroux, 1997). The fundamental aim of critical pedagogy is to construct schools and education as "agents of change." Through schools, critical pedagogy attempts to build more egalitarian power relations, to strengthen the voices of learners, and to inspire critical consciousness, in order to promote social change. These are noble goals. Yet, to think of it seriously, the idea (or ideal) of schools-for-social-change is quite an ambitious quest. It seems even out of touch with reality, especially given the neoliberal currents that have swept education in recent years. The talk today is about efficiency, accountability, competition, and standard testing. The idea of schools as change agents is not exactly the topic of the day.

With such challenges from both within and without, can critical pedagogy really achieve this lofty call for social change?

This question is more pertinent to ask, as there have been serious critiques on critical pedagogy. For instance, Peter McLaren, once a chief proponent of critical pedagogy, has declared that critical pedagogy is no longer viable in instigating social change. McLaren claims that critical pedagogy "no longer serve[s] as an adequate social or pedagogical platform from which to mount a vigorous challenge to the current social division of labor and its effects on the socially reproductive function of schooling in late capitalist society" (McLaren, 1998: 448). This is a serious blow, since critical pedagogy was formulated precisely to pursue a "language of possibility." So, why do we have such serious criticism, which challenges the very identity of critical pedagogy?

This book critically examines the "language of possibility" of critical pedagogy, and problematizes critical pedagogy's claim to be the "language of possibility." There are several reasons why we need a closer examination of the "language of possibility," and the idea of school as a change agent. To begin with, almost three decades have passed since the emergence of critical pedagogy. So, it seems like the right time to ask ourselves how critical pedagogy has been doing in its search for the possibilities. What possibilities has critical pedagogy presented so far? How real and effective are the alternatives that critical pedagogy has presented? How many dents can they make in the social reality? In a way, this book is a reality and status check for critical pedagogy.

Also, the field of critical pedagogy, due to its interdisciplinary and multidisciplinary nature, embodies a broad range of theoretical perspectives. As such, there are diverse (sometimes conflicting) ideas and approaches to the "language of possibility." While we may say that we all pursue a pedagogy of possibility/hope/transformation, it is possible that we may be talking about different ideas. So, it is not at all clear what we imagine when we talk about a pedagogy of possibility/hope/ transformation, and what kind of society we imagine when we talk about social change. As I will show in later chapters, many varying pedagogies have been suggested as alternatives within critical pedagogy. In a sense, this number of positions can be problematic, because it can create confusion. Thus, I believe that there is a strong need to put together these various ideas and approaches to "possibilities." By analyzing and synthesizing various ideas, this book intends to identify and critically examine different formulations for making schools agencies of social change.

Furthermore, contrary to critical pedagogy's claim to present a "language of possibility," I believe that the possibilities in critical pedagogy are not sufficiently articulated. The possibilities are often presented in broad and abstract terms, such as equality, social justice, democracy, care, and utopia. Needless to say, these ideas and principles are important to critical pedagogy, and it is certainly crucial to have an in-depth and critical understanding of these principles. However, very little is done to formulate these principles into more concrete forms of alternative education. Therefore, there is a need to identify or extract alternative projects from abstract ideas of critical pedagogy, and more importantly, to critically examine them. How is the "language of possibility" conceptualized? What are the underlying politics of critical pedagogy? What alternative visions of schooling does critical pedagogy truly offer against mainstream education? Will the alternatives bring the social changes that critical pedagogy strives for? What does a vision of social change really mean? What kinds of social changes are we talking about? These are the questions this book addresses.

The goals of this book are two-fold. The first goal is to critically examine the "language of possibility" of critical pedagogy. For this goal, the book first presents an analysis on the historical and theoretical contexts of critical pedagogy. This analysis is necessary in order to understand why critical pedagogy has pursued its "language of possibility" in certain directions and not others. Based on the analysis, this book synthesizes various ideas and approaches in critical pedagogy, and argues that there are four main alternative projects in critical pedagogy. These four alternative projects are then critically examined. For each project, the theoretical frameworks and political orientations are investigated, the underlying assumptions are scrutinized, the key contentions and controversies are explored, and the limitations are analyzed. Based on this synthesis and analysis, this book argues that, although critical pedagogy claims to impact and change society, the inherent limitations present within the dominant discourses of critical pedagogy are what stifle the possibility of social change. For this reason, the book argues that critical pedagogy, as it is, will at best modernize, rather than change, the system. As this book argues that critical pedagogy is narrow and lopsided in its pursuit of the "language of possibility," the second goal of the book is to explore how to overcome or compensate for these shortcomings of critical pedagogy. The second part of this book explores and presents "other" alternatives that have been missing or marginalized in the mainstream of critical pedagogy. For that, the book examines the recent critical education literature, particularly related to globalization.

Contributions to the Field

The literature in critical pedagogy can be classified into three categories: the theoretical, the pedagogical, and the political. The first category is *theoretical* studies. These studies focus on critical theories, which constitute the foundation of critical pedagogy. Many consider Paulo Freire as the founder of critical pedagogy; however, critical pedagogy embodies various theories. Although there are some commonalities, different theoretical orientations sometimes generate different kinds or emphases of critical pedagogy. Much critical pedagogy literature introduces various core theories that underlie critical pedagogy, such as the Frankfurt critical theory, the respective theories of Gramsci, Althusser, and Freire, neo-Marxist theory, poststructural theories, postmodern theories, feminist theories, and postcolonial theories (Ellsworth, 1988/1992; Lather, 1991; Luke & Gore, 1992; Zavarzadeh & Morton, 1994; McLaren, 1995; Morrow & Torres, 2002; Kincheloe, 2004; Gur-Ze'ev, 2007).

The second category is *pedagogical* studies. This literature focuses on the micro-level of pedagogy. The focus of this literature is how to use critical pedagogy in classrooms. The major areas of this work are what to teach and how to teach, with the aim to explore more democratic and critical forms of knowledge, and more democratic pedagogical arrangements and school cultures (Shor, 1992; hooks, 1994; Rethinking Schools, 1994; McLaren, 1997; Elenes, 2003; Wrigley, 2006). There are a wide range of studies in this category. There are studies that apply critical pedagogy to various subjects, not only to subjects that seem relevant (such as history and social studies), but also to subjects that seem not to be explicitly relevant (such as math and science) (Gilbert, 2011). These studies cover all levels of education, from kindergarten to college. In addition, studies are done to practice/apply critical pedagogy in various countries.

The third category is *political* studies. This literature is a critical analysis on issues and problems that influence the policies and practices of education. This covers a wide range of issues, such as global capitalism (Allman, 2001; Apple et al., 2005; Fischman et al., 2005; McLaren, 2005; Cote et al., 2007; Spring, 2007), neoliberalism (Apple, 2001; Giroux, 2004; McLaren & Jaramillo, 2007), race (Leonardo, 2002, 2005; Allen, 2004; Darder & Torres, 2004; Grande, 2004; Watkins, 2005; Bernal et al., 2006; Liou & Antrop-González, 2011; Orelus, 2011), gender and sexuality (Ellsworth, 1988/1992; Luke & Gore, 1992; Weiler & Mitchell, 1992; Macdonald & Sancher-Casal, 2002; Fine, 2003; Hickman, 2011), mass media, popular culture, and technology (Duncan-Andrade & Morrell, 2007; Suoranta & Vadén, 2007; Carroll-Miranda, 2011; Kress & DeGennaro, 2011), high-stakes testing (Janesick, 2007), and urban schools (Anyon, 2005; Duncan-Andrade & Morrell, 2008).

This categorization is only a conceptual tool to help us grasp the boundaries and directions of critical pedagogy. In reality, many studies do not belong to just one category. In fact, most critical pedagogy literature usually includes theoretical foundations, even when the focus is on either the pedagogical or political dimension. There is, however, one more dimension that does not belong to the above three categories. It is what I call "meta-analysis" on the critical pedagogy as a field—on the goal and scope of critical pedagogy itself. What is the goal of critical pedagogy, or what should it be? What should critical pedagogy do, focus on, and strive for? In the late 1980s and early 1990s, there were serious debates on the question of whether and how critical pedagogy could be power-free and genuinely empowering. These debates were basically back-and-forth exchanges between neo-Marxism and poststructuralism, in the form of feminist poststructuralists (Ellsworth, 1988/1992; Lather, 1992, 1998; Luke & Gore, 1992) criticizing the critical pedagogy theories that were dominated by male neo-Marxists (Giroux, 1988a; McLaren, 1988). In essence, this was a theoretical level of discussion focusing on which theory (neo-Marxism or poststructuralism) was a better theoretical framework for critical pedagogy.

Recently, though, there seems to be a growing movement to revisit the goals and scope of critical pedagogy. This time, the driving impetus is a different one—globalization. In the last decade or so, there has been a growing awareness of globalization, and it has finally started to make its impact on critical pedagogy. Now there are growing studies on how critical pedagogy could and should deal with neoliberal globalization (Allman, 2001; Apple, 2001; Giroux, 2004; Apple et al., 2005; Fischman et al., 2005; McLaren, 2005; Cote et al., 2007; Gur-Ze'ev, 2007; McLaren & Jaramillo, 2007; Spring, 2007). Ideas such as utopian pedagogy (Peters & Freeman-Moir, 2006; Cote et al., 2007) and place-based pedagogy (Gruenewald & Smith, 2007; Martin & Riele, 2011) have been presented, and new theoretical frameworks from neo- and post-colonial theories (e.g., revival of Franz Fanon) introduced into critical pedagogy (Duncan-Andrade & Morrell, 2008; Lissovoy, 2008; Leonardo & Porter, 2010).

This book belongs to the meta-analysis category. It examines what critical pedagogy should do, focus on, and strive for. It is a theoretical analysis, or meta-analysis, on the "language of possibility" with the aim of extracting and critically examining its philosophical elaboration and its alternatives. Yet, this book is different from other works in two ways: first in its question, and second in its methods. First, this book is unique in the very questions it addresses: what are the alternative projects of critical pedagogy, and are these alternative projects critical enough? Somewhat surprisingly, there exists no study, as far as I know, that synthesizes and critically analyzes the projects of critical pedagogy as a whole—what alternatives critical pedagogy presents, and what kinds of politics inform and underlie critical pedagogy. Most studies, as reviewed above, focus on a single dimension (e.g., globalization, race, or the Frankfurt School). This book, somewhat ambitiously, offers a meta-analysis of the very idea of critical pedagogy as the "language of possibility." It surveys the broad dimensions of critical pedagogy, with a single focus on the very idea of critical pedagogy as a change agent or as the "language of possibility." Critical pedagogy aligns various projects within differing formations, each with their own trajectory. This book examines how critical pedagogy formulates its projects, and what influences its scopes, approaches, and directions.

Second, this book is unique in its method/approach—historical analysis and political economy. As mentioned above, the debates between feminists and male critical pedagogists in the 1980s and 1990s were theoretical disputes. The recent literature on the nature and goals of critical pedagogy still focuses largely on theoretical investigations. Unlike this abstract theoretical approach, this book analyzes concrete projects—what should critical schools/education look like and do? To put it differently, what this book is trying to do is to concretize abstract ideals and suggestive remarks into reality-based systemic forms. In doing so, this book examines how critical pedagogy has evolved and formulated its political positions within the larger historical context of economic, political, social, and cultural changes. Many ideas in critical pedagogy are a reflection of, and in line with, the larger trends and shifts in academia and the politics of the new social movements and the New Left. Thus, in order to have a thorough understanding of core concepts of critical pedagogy, I believe it is crucial to understand the context from which these concepts came.

Qualifications and Limitations

Before I move on, I need to put forward some qualifications at the outset. As much as it is helpful to present what this book is trying to do, I believe it is also helpful to clarify what this book is *not* trying to do. First, this book is not intended to provide "practical" guidelines for how to practice critical pedagogy. There are several books and studies about how to practice critical pedagogy in classrooms. As stated above, this book is about identifying alternative projects within critical pedagogy. The reason I focus on the "language of possibility" is because I want to extract more realistic and concrete alternatives from the theory- and abstract-ideas-ridden discourses of critical pedagogy. That is also why I intentionally use the term "project." In that sense, one can say this book is an effort to concretize the ideas of critical pedagogy. Concretization can contribute to a practical dimension, but what is concrete is not necessarily practical.

Second, this book neither reviews theoretical foundations of critical pedagogy, nor explains core concepts of critical pedagogy. There are several books that do that already. Of course, this book examines the diverse theories that underlie critical pedagogy as they are related to the "language of possibility." However, its aim is not to explain foundational theories of critical pedagogy. Rather, this book is an analysis of theories of the "language of possibility." As such, I write this book with the expectation that readers have some familiarity with the basic concepts and theories of critical pedagogy.

Third, this book does not aim to present an alternative to critical pedagogy. The goal of this book, as stated above, is to analyze and synthesize various alternatives that are presented within critical pedagogy. Obviously, the intention of such analysis is to give suggestions and directions to our search for alternative visions of education. I hope this book will provide some general directions and implications for critical pedagogy, but this book does not intend to present an/my alternative model of critical education. In other words, this book examines where we have been, so that we may be able to get our future direction right.

And finally, this book does not cover all critical pedagogy studies. The critical pedagogy I analyze in this book is limited to literature written in English. And my analysis—its theoretical orientations, political positions, and trends of discourse—is situated in the current historical and cultural context of the United States. I assume that there are general commonalities within critical pedagogy in other countries. However, I also think that critical pedagogy could have somewhat different approaches and meanings in other countries, depending on the social, political, and cultural context of a specific society. As we know, the meaning of a discourse is dependent on the discourse field. So, I do not claim that my understanding and analysis on critical pedagogy in this book is universal or relevant globally.

Overview of Chapters

Chapter 2 presents the historical context of critical pedagogy, and explores the origin of critical pedagogy—why and how critical pedagogy emerged in the 1980s. The origin is important to understand, because it has shaped what critical pedagogy is and how it has formulated projects to make schools agencies of change. The chapter investigates various push and pull factors that have influenced critical pedagogy, by sorting them into the Foe (mainstream education), the Counterpart (neo-Marxism), the Savior (Paulo Freire), the Contour (postmodernism), the Contender (feminism), and the Challenger (anti-racism and postcolonialism). It concludes with the boundary questions: How do we decide which ones are critical pedagogy and which ones are not? Who are critical pedagogues and who are not? In other words, how should we decide the boundary of critical pedagogy, and why does it matter?

Chapter 3 provides an analysis on the theoretical context of critical pedagogy. It focuses on the broad historical background of the emergence of cultural studies and cultural politics. In recent years, cultural theories have had significant influence on critical educational theories. Why did culture come to the forefront of academic studies and of the politics of the New Left? How did culture become so important? What were the political and economic contexts that catalyzed this move? What problems do these theories address that were not addressed before? This chapter explores these questions and examines the political economy of cultural theories/politics.

Chapter 4 identifies and critically examines the main alternative projects that are presented by mainstream critical pedagogy. It first presents two main agendas that critical pedagogy focuses on: transformation of knowledge (curriculum) and pedagogy (in a narrow sense, i.e., teaching). It highlights how critical pedagogy is similar and different from the neo-Marxist education theories. Based on that, the chapter identifies four alternative projects that are dominant in critical pedagogy, which I call the "project of experience," the "project of multiplicity and inclusion," the "project of anti-hierarchy democracy," and the "project of individual enlightenment." These four projects are closely examined for their theoretical bases and orientations, their controversies and contentions, and their limitations and problems.

Chapters 2 to 4 are devoted to critically examining the "language of possibility" of critical pedagogy, and to demonstrating the narrow and lopsided approach of critical pedagogy. Based on that, the next two chapters are attempts to go beyond the boundary of the "language of possibility" of the mainstream critical pedagogy, in order to compensate, to correct, to widen, and to expand the horizon of our thinking for alternative and critical education.

Chapter 5 focuses on recent education literature on globalization as another important venue in exploring the "language of possibility." More than other issues, globalization has pushed education studies to come up with projects of resistance to global capitalism. This chapter identifies five major issues/problems that critical education is addressing—(1) TINA (There Is No Alternative), (2) instrumentalism and dehumanization, (3) single global culture (universalism), (4) global capitalism, and (5) Western colonization—and five corresponding alternative positions that have been presented as their solutions: utopianism, humanism, localism, globalism, and postcolonialism.

Chapter 6 takes up the larger and final question. If critical pedagogy claims to be an agent of social change, what kind of society are we striving for? Most critical pedagogy literature presents some basic principles, such as social justice, equality, and democracy. Yet, lacking are more real/concrete forms of social systems. If we are against neoliberal global capitalism, are we striving for socialism or the betterment of capitalism? Should we be anti-globalization, or counter-globalization? Would it be a globalized democratic system or localized forms of democratic societies? As a way to handle this question, the chapter overviews several anti-systemic alternatives presented by several theories: (1) reformists: social democracy with welfare state; (2) globalists: global socialism and supernational politics; (3) localists: autarchy and earth democracy; and (4) mixed economy of public and private. The chapter concludes by highlighting some fundamental contentions within these alternatives.

Chapter 7, the conclusion, attempts to locate the contribution of my study in the field of critical pedagogy at large. Then, it recaps the major arguments of this book. It elaborates on the points of my analysis on critical pedagogy: nonpoliticization, liberal/reformist tendency, moralism, culture and postmodernism, micro-level approaches, and idealistic tendencies. It concludes by laying out some basic principles, and sketches future directions for critical education.

2

THE HISTORICAL CONTEXT
The Origin of Critical Pedagogy

Introduction

Not all of the core ideas of critical pedagogy are brand new. Like any other new perspective, critical pedagogy is built on previous theories and ideas. For example, the idea of constructing knowledge *with* students was already present more than 100 years ago in John Dewey's idea of "experience" (Dewey, 1902/1938), and more recently in constructivism (Vygotsky, 1978, 1997). The idea of schools as change agents is not new either. In the early 20th century, social reconstructionism was based precisely on the idea that schools can and should effect social change. It was powerfully presented in George Counts' book *Dare the School Build a New Social Order?* (1932). More recently, we can find the same idea in the civil rights movement and theories of multicultural education. True, one may say that critical pedagogy is more overtly political than the progressive education movement, constructivism, or multicultural education. Yet, it is undeniable that there are some similarities among these educational theories. Furthermore, some core ideas of critical pedagogy are comparable with the indigenous belief systems of the Native Americans (Grande, 2004).

Certainly, there were individual teachers who were actually practicing critical pedagogy in their classrooms well before the term critical pedagogy was invented! Why, then, was this new name, "critical pedagogy," coined? What were the historical contexts that gave birth to critical pedagogy? If many of its ideas are not new, where can we draw the boundaries for critical pedagogy? This chapter explores the historical context for the origin of critical pedagogy: why and how critical pedagogy emerged in the 1980s. The origin is important to understand, because it has shaped what critical pedagogy is and has become—its identities, its foci, its agendas, its politics, and its projects. This chapter examines several historical forces that have shaped and influenced the politics and projects of critical pedagogy.

The Foe: Mainstream Education Paradigm

One good way to understand what critical pedagogy is *for* is to figure out what it is *against*. It is apparent that critical pedagogy is in opposition to the mainstream education paradigm. If there are various and diverse perspectives within the mainstream education paradigm (from conservative to neoliberal), then what exactly is critical pedagogy against? Numerous critiques bedevil the mainstream education paradigm, from its model of "banking education" to the irrelevance of its curriculum, from its reliance on standardized testing to its undemocratic school culture and its toleration of discrimination and inequality. The list could go on, since there are many real differences between the mainstream education paradigm and critical pedagogy on many aspects of education: from curriculum, instruction, evaluation, and classroom management, to school culture.

These differences stem from how each paradigm views the roles and functions of schools as social institutions in relation to the larger society. By and large, critical pedagogy and critical education theories reject two major premises of the mainstream education paradigm. The first premise that critical pedagogy challenges is the idea of schools as the "great equalizer." From the inception of the public school system in the U.S. from the 1840s to 1880s, schools have largely been considered meritocratic institutions, which provide equal and fair opportunities to all. Regardless of family backgrounds, students have the same chance to succeed in schools, and thus in society. Schools are egalitarian institutions, it is argued, especially as compared to economic, political, cultural, military, religious, and other social institutions. It is not that the dominant education paradigm does not acknowledge the unequal outcomes of schooling. According to this perspective, the unequal outcomes may be unfortunate, but they are inevitable, natural, or even desirable, due to the different abilities of individuals—either innate or environmental (roughly, this is the conservative's position). Others acknowledge that discrimination against and disadvantages still exist for some groups, for instance women, minorities, and the poor within the school system. However, discrimination is considered the exception, and the rule is that schools are still based on equality and meritocracy (this is roughly the liberal's position).

Critical education theories, including critical pedagogy, reject or at least challenge this "equalizer thesis." To begin with, they point out that schools have never provided equal opportunities to all, although educational opportunities have expanded over time. And even with equal (or more equal) opportunities, they point out that there are various mechanisms in schools (i.e., tracking) that discriminate against some children who are considered to be the "others." Some go even further and argue (e.g., Apple, 1982; Spring, 1989) that the idea of "equal opportunity" is based on notions of inequalities. In other words, equal opportunities are given to create unequal outcomes, to sort between the "leaders" and "followers." So, Joel Spring argues that schools are a sorting machine, rather than an equalizer (Spring, 1989, 2008a). To critical education theorists (such as Apple and Spring), not only do schools not provide equal opportunities to all, but they also perform the double function of (1) reproducing and magnifying the existing inequalities; and (2) legitimizing this reproduction (more on this in the next section). That said, critical pedagogues hold differing opinions as to whether or not schools actually play an active role in the reproduction of inequalities. Some critical pedagogues agree with the liberal's position, which sees the outcome of inequalities in school as the exception (a fault, or an imperfection of the school system). However, there are other critical pedagogues who see the reproduction of inequalities in the schools as the rule, not the exception. To them, schools are set up or designed to (re)produce unequal outcomes. Therefore, inequalities are not "unintended" outcomes. To put it another way, there is a more liberal version of critical pedagogy and a more radical version of critical pedagogy.

The second idea to which critical pedagogy objects is instrumental reasoning, which is fundamental and prevalent in the mainstream education paradigm. One essential perspective in the mainstream education paradigm is seeing schooling as a means to an end, both for individuals (getting a better job) and for society (economic development or nation building). Of course, there are multiple dimensions to the instrumental approach to schooling. For instance, knowledge taught and learned at schools is basically seen as a means to pass a test, and the test scores as a means to enter better universities or colleges, which, in turn, are only means to getting better-paid jobs in the labor market. For the overwhelming majority of the general public, the simple truth is that they go to school to get credentials, which are believed to lead to better jobs. In the modern capitalist society, almost everything becomes a means to an end, the end being profits. We not only sell our labor and credentials, but also our personalities, manners, attitudes, and smiles. The modern school institutions have emerged with the modern state and modern society, which are based on instrumental rationality. Because this instrumental reasoning is so prevalent in our society as well as in our schools, it is sometimes hard to recognize and decipher it in our daily lives.

Critical pedagogy criticizes the instrumental rationality and reification that dominates the schools and the society at large, which leads to dehumanization and oppression. The critical education paradigm tries to transform schools for humanization and for social change. Some people may argue that critical pedagogy also sees schooling as a means to an end, only the end being different from the mainstream paradigm. In this case, the end is social change or building a better society. This is a rather

THE ORIGIN OF CRITICAL PEDAGOGY   19

simple and literal understanding of "instrumental rationality." Yet, looking at it this way, what distinguishes critical pedagogy from the mainstream education paradigm would be the end that the schools ought to serve. While the mainstream perspective views schools basically as institutions to maintain (via improvements and reforms) the existing social system, critical pedagogy views schools as social institutions that should seek to change the society. This difference in the way the mainstream education paradigm and critical education paradigm envision the role of schools is ultimately due to how each of them views the society at large. If one views the society as equal and just, the role of schools within that society would be to socialize its members in order to maintain and reproduce their stable society. But if one sees the society as unequal and unjust, then the role of schools in that society would not be to maintain and reproduce the existing unstable social system, but to change it for the better.

Out of these fundamental differences, the two paradigms construct different approaches to many aspects of schooling and education. In general, the mainstream paradigm approaches education with a technocratic framework (i.e., focusing on the "hows"). It treats educational issues—curriculum, teaching, learning, evaluation, discipline, and classroom management— as both technical and nonpolitical, and thus has focused on coming up with procedural models (Apple, 1979; Giroux, 1983; Posner, 2004). In opposition, the critical education paradigm has highlighted power, and thus focuses much more on the political dimensions of education, schooling, and pedagogy. In short, the mainstream paradigm frames educational issues as technical problems, while critical education/pedagogy frames them as political problems.

The Counterpart: Neo-Marxism

New perspectives, as Immanuel Wallerstein points out, are better understood if we think of them as "a protest against older perspectives" (Wallerstein, 2004a: 1). This is true for critical pedagogy. Critical pedagogy has a counterpart, which it is protesting against. That counterpart is the earlier critical theories, especially neo-Marxist theories of education (sometimes called "conflict" theories, as a way to hide the taboo term "Marxist"). So, what is it about neo-Marxist education theories that critical pedagogy is protesting against? Many have written about neo-Marxist theories of education, so this chapter will only present the core ideas of neo-Marxist education theories, so as to highlight what reactions critical pedagogy has had to them, and how these reactions have shaped the very identity of critical pedagogy.

During the post-civil rights era, a renewed interest in critically examining the larger roles of schools in the capitalist society emerged. Various types of macro-theory emerged during the 1970s in the quest to explain the relationship between education and the wider social structure. Among those, one of the most influential has been the work of Bowles and Gintis (1976). Contrary to the common/liberal belief that schools reduce inequalities, they maintain that education in a capitalist society (in the U.S. in this case) reproduces fundamental economic inequalities. Bowles and Gintis have been particularly successful in launching an effective critique on the liberal ideology of education. Through this, they provide an important basis to develop a relational, political and economic analysis on schooling.

However, their work has some limitations, as many have already pointed out. The key problem of Bowles and Gintis' theory is its economic determinism. By basing their work on Marxist materialism, Bowles and Gintis largely neglect the aspect of ideology. Also, their deterministic theory does not and cannot explain the inherent contradictory mechanism. To be fair, they are aware of the contradictions in the reproduction process:

> Of course the use of the educational system to legitimize inequality is not without its own problems. Ideologies and structures which serve to hide and preserve one form of injustice often provide the basis of an assault on another. The ideology of equal educational opportunity and meritocracy is precisely such a contradictory mechanism.
>
> (Bowles & Gintis, 1976: 103)

However, they do little to articulate the contradictions both in the "base" and in the "superstructure." Furthermore, Bowles and Gintis treat the curriculum and inner workings of schools as either irrelevant or as a side issue (Apple, 1979). As Karabel and Halsey have pointed out, "despite some insight into the non-cognitive aspects of the educational process, they [Bowles and Gintis] have largely allowed the internal workings of schools to remain [in] a black box" (Karabel & Halsey, 1977: 44).

Subsequent critical education theories have tried to respond to these limitations of Bowles and Gintis' work. Some scholars, while accepting Bowles and Gintis' assertion that schools (re)produce the existing social and economic structures, have ventured to actually explain how the reproduction process occurs. These critical educational theorists have employed the works of Gramsci, Althusser, and Stuart Hall, and have introduced new concepts into the study of education, such as cultural capital, hidden curriculum, ideology/hegemony, and schools as a state apparatus (Bourdieu & Passeron, 1977; Apple, 1979,

1982; Dale et al., 1981; Giroux, 1983, 1988b; Carnoy & Levin, 1985). The main claim of these works is that the school, as a part of the culture/superstructure, plays a significant role in (re)producing and legitimizing the hegemony of a capitalist society. Schools and education accomplish this through several mechanisms by:

1. choosing to include or exclude certain knowledge from the curriculum;
2. conveying certain, but not other, norms and values to students (hidden curriculum); and
3. utilizing certain social interactions and practices to sort out students for future careers.

Neo-Marxist theories have been very successful in providing powerful critiques of schooling. There is no doubt as to their contributions in education. However, what they have not been very successful at, and thus have been frequently criticized for, is presenting feasible alternatives: examples of schools for social change. It is this lack of alternatives that prompted the emergence of critical pedagogy in the 1980s. The proponents of critical pedagogy criticize earlier neo-Marxist theories of education, arguing that they provide only a "language of critique." If education and politics are primarily determined by the economy, as argued by Bowles and Gintis (1976), many educators lament that there is little that could be done in schools to change society in any fundamental way (except, of course, an economic revolution of sorts). One of the major limitations of Bowles and Gintis' correspondence theory, it was argued, was that it portrayed the capitalist system as all powerful and thus underplayed agency and resistance (this is where Paul

Willis, Michael Apple, and Henry Giroux entered the scene). As a way to overcome this economic determinism and aporia, critical pedagogy began a move away from focusing on the economy and toward focusing on culture (a point I will return to in Chapter 3).

In summation, critical pedagogy emerged as a reaction to, or as a corrective effort against, the economic (and cultural) determinism of earlier critical theories. By introducing the possibility of human agency and resistance, critical pedagogues attempted to develop not only a pedagogy of critique, but also to build a pedagogy of hope. Fundamentally, the aim of critical pedagogy is to correct the deterministic and pessimistic conclusions of neo-Marxist theories, and to transform a "language of critique" into a "language of possibility" (Giroux, 1997: 108).

The Savior: Paulo Freire

From where, then, did critical pedagogy find the "language of possibility" and pedagogy of hope? Critical pedagogues turned to and drew from various theories and perspectives: the Frankfurt School, existentialism, humanism, poststructuralism, postmodernism, and postcolonialism. Many would agree, however, that it was from Paulo Freire that critical pedagogues ultimately found the language of hope: "[It is w]ith Freire, the notion of critical pedagogy as we understand it today emerges" (Kincheloe, 2004: 69). Freire's most influential book, *Pedagogy of the Oppressed*, written in 1968, has been distributed globally in many languages since the 1970s. The ideas in this book impacted labor and community movements in many parts of the world. Freire's book was particularly influential in the Third (underdeveloped) World, where oppression was more severe, and thus the oppositional struggles against undemocratic political regimes more urgent. However, in the U.S. and the rest of the First (developed) World, Freire's influence was different. Lacking radical movements, his pedagogy was often utilized by educators in a de-politicized form, as a technique, or a method of teaching (Allman, 1999; Kincheloe, 2004).

In a way, critical pedagogy played a crucial role in reviving interest in Freire. Since much has already been written, generally, on Freire and his pedagogy, this chapter will focus on only two questions relevant to this book: why did critical pedagogy turn to Freire, and what influences did Freire have on shaping the identity and projects of critical pedagogy? One simple and obvious reason is because Freire offered the elements of hope and possibility. While other critical theories focused mainly on critiquing, Freire presented a transformative pedagogy, which could lead to liberation. In other words, he focused not only on deconstruction, but also on (re)construction. Thus, Kincheloe calls Freire "critical pedagogy's prophet of hope" (Kincheloe, 2004: 72). Rather than viewing schools as a mechanism of social control and reproduction, Freire argued that education could be liberatory even within the most limiting circumstances. He saw education as the practice of developing a critical perception of reality among learners/participants, which could effectively lead to what he called "conscientization."

Freire's pedagogical principles are centered on the transformation of individuals, or individual consciousness, from a fatal acceptance of oppression/reality to a critical consciousness/hope that reality can be changed for the better. This transformation is possible, according to Freire, because it is our human and historical vocation to become more fully human (Freire, 1970/1997). In other words, the basis of hope and possibility to

Freire is human destiny, or human nature for "humanization." And because of this inevitable vocation to be fully human, once we are awakened, Freire argued, we have no choice but to eliminate oppression, which prohibits our potential for full humanization.

Another reason why Freire appealed to critical pedagogy was because he offered "not just a narrative but also a methodology of liberation" (Lissovoy, 2008: 11), with steps to follow, which he called "a methodology of conscientização" (Freire, 1970/1997: 85). Freire built his theory of transformative pedagogy on actual projects: the literacy campaigns that started in Brazil and later expanded to Chile, Guinea Bissau, Nicaragua, and elsewhere. In *Pedagogy of the Oppressed*, Freire carefully delineates what needs to be done in order to develop and implement a liberatory pedagogy. Although Freire cautioned against blindly importing his methods, one of his strengths is the fact that he showed how his problem-solving education (the pedagogy of transformation) can be practiced with participants.

While Freire offered a pedagogy of hope and transformation, there are some challenges and problems in adopting Freire in critical pedagogy. One challenge is the Marxist basis in Freire's thinking, which often eludes readers, as Paula Allman (1999) rightly points out. Freire's key concepts—history, humanization, critical (dialectical) perception of reality, and the relationship between the object and the subject—cannot be correctly comprehended without background knowledge and understanding of Marxism. One cannot fully comprehend the foundation of Freire's pedagogy of liberation if one does not grasp why Freire considers "the fundamental theme of our epoch to be that of *domination*" (Freire, 1970/1997: 84, original emphasis), and why he claims that the limit-situation of our epoch is that "in which people are reduced to things" (ibid.). If one does not see that Freire is referring to "thingfication" or reification, one cannot understand the oppression or liberation, which is the fundamental concept in Freire's pedagogy. In fact, it is not at all uncommon for students to struggle with grasping the concept of "oppression" when reading Freire. "Who are the oppressors?" they ask. Sometimes, oppression is trivialized and de-politicized as difficulties all of us experience at one time or another in our lives. This, however, is based on the misunderstanding that everyone becomes the oppressed or that one becomes both the oppressed and the oppressor, which is an absurd reading of Freire. This lack of knowledge of Marxism is, as Allman (1999) argues, why Freire has been so often misunderstood and misapplied as just a teaching method. Unfortunately, this misunderstanding and misuse of Freire still can be seen in some critical pedagogy literature.

There are other issues with how the utilization of Freire has directed critical pedagogy in certain directions. Since Freire's main focus was on transforming the consciousness of individuals, critical pedagogy focused on individualized projects (a point I will return to in Chapter 4). Also, Freire heavily emphasized the importance of cultural action in producing social change. In other words, his interest was in cultural revolution, not political revolution or institutional revolution. This emphasis on cultural action and cultural revolution influenced and directed critical pedagogy toward cultural politics. That said, it should be noted that the dominance of cultural politics in critical pedagogy is not exclusively due to the influence of Freire. Rather, this "cultural turn" was a general trend that influenced Left politics and academics since the 1970s (elaborated on in

Chapter 3). As such, I think it is important to understand that Freire was himself influenced by the trends of his time.

In addition, there is an issue regarding the relationship between pedagogical projects and political projects. Freire sees pedagogical projects as an essential part of political projects, yet he also makes clear that pedagogical projects (critical perception of reality) do not necessarily lead to political transformation. He says, "[critical perception of reality] is necessary, but not a sufficient condition by itself for liberation ... The oppressed can overcome the contradiction in which they are caught only when this perception enlists them in the struggle to free themselves" (Freire, 1970/1997: 31). Yet, because of his focus on pedagogical projects, it is easy to neglect other conditions for liberation, which in turn can thwart the discussion of how pedagogical projects could actually lead to political projects. If critical pedagogy limits itself exclusively to pedagogical projects, it leaves out other potential projects schools could contemplate and should pursue.

Although many regard Paulo Freire as a founder of and a key figure in critical pedagogy, there are differing views as to Freire's location within critical pedagogy. For some, critical pedagogy is all about Freire; it begins with him and ends with him. To them, Freire *is* critical pedagogy, and critical pedagogy *is* Freire. Others view Freire as one of many who inform and shape critical pedagogy. To them, critical pedagogy is more than Freire. In a way, this difference is a reflection of the tension between the identities and boundaries of critical pedagogy. Some people see critical pedagogy as mainly about teaching (pedagogy in the narrow sense), and thus focus on the micro-level. On the other hand, there are those who see critical pedagogy more on a macro-level, focusing on the broader power relationships between schooling and society. To put it differently, the micro-position (critical pedagogy is Freire) gives its credence to critical *pedagogy*, while the macro-position (critical pedagogy is beyond Freire) emphasizes *critical* pedagogy. Overall, I think critical pedagogy is more geared toward the micro-level. After all, this is why critical pedagogy rebelled against earlier Marxist education theories.

In the end, while Freire is widely considered as the prophet of hope and thus a founder or savior of critical pedagogy, there are some basic questions about what concrete influences Freire has had on critical pedagogy. Is he more a symbolic figure for the possibility of hope? Did he really save critical pedagogy from pessimistic conclusions? Is the liberatory education presented in his problem-solving pedagogy the answer for alternative visions of schooling that critical pedagogues are looking for? Did Freirean theory and pedagogy present concrete alternatives to the mainstream and neoliberal education paradigm?

The Contour: Postmodernism

At the time when critical pedagogy theorists were trying to find an alternative education ("language of possibility") apart from and beyond neo-Marxist education theories, a sea of change was surging in critical theories. Since the late 1970s, critical theories have been moving away from Marxism (or a version of Marxism, called by various names such as structural Marxism, material Marxism, orthodox Marxism, or vulgar Marxism), and new kinds of critical theories have begun to get more circulation. This was the rise of the post-theories: poststructuralism, postmodernism, and postcolonialism. And critical pedagogy was heavily influenced and shaped by this wave of change. In fact, it would have been a surprise if it had remained uninfluenced or untouched. One qualification, however, is necessary here. Some people make a distinction between poststructuralism and post-modernism, and treat them differently (there are some subtle differences), while others do not distinguish between the two (there are some fundamental commonalities). For the purpose of this book, I treat them together, and use poststructuralism and postmodernism interchangeably.

Chapter 3 covers the historical contexts behind the emergence of postmodernism in the 1970s, so here I will only highlight two key influences of postmodernism that have contributed to critical pedagogy. One key influence of postmodernism on critical pedagogy is multiple marginalities. Countering the class-centered approach of Marxist theories, poststructuralism argues that there is no one center. Rather, there are multiple marginalities, such as gender, race, sexuality, disability, religion, national origin, and so on. And according to postmodernism, the significance of any marginality is contextual, not predeter-mined. In one context, race may be the most significant, while in another context, sexuality may be. For some, gender may be the most significant marginality, while for others it may be disability. The recognition of multiplicity and heterogeneity brought forth the need for inclusivity in critical theories. This is why feminists and some anti-race theorists are drawn to poststructuralism and postmodernism. However, multiplicity opened up a host of sticky questions. If there are multiple marginalities, what are the relationships among them? If the significance of each marginality is contextual, is there any way to know whether some marginalities are more significant than others? Are all marginalities equally significant, or does it all depend on their contexts? If it depends, then are we falling into relativism? If all a theory can say is "it depends," then what is the use of that theory? We have been debating these questions for some time.

The other contribution of postmodernism is a new understanding of subject formation. Contrary to Marxist theories, poststructuralism sees subject formation as much more complex, indeterminate, and loose. According to poststructuralists, subject formation involves more than ideology and consciousness (ideas and beliefs), also involving feelings and desires (see Kincheloe, 2004). Therefore, subjects are not only more complex, but also more fragmented, floating, and indeterminate. Poststructuralists' keen attention to subject formation —infusing concepts from psychoanalysis—provided a sensibility to other forces (more than class) that shape our subjects. Again, this was a much-welcomed idea for feminists and anti-racism scholars.

However, there exists an irony in the marriage between postmodernism and critical pedagogy. At its core, postmodernism is a discourse of suspicion/incredulity or impossibility. On the one hand, postmodernism rejects the Enlightenment projects of modernism. On the other hand, however, postmodernism is skeptical and critiques the revolutionary projects of Marxism (they call Marxism a "high" modernism). So, it is an interesting twist that the quest of critical pedagogy (for a "language of possibility") ended up with and at postmodernism (a discourse of suspicion). How to combine these two seemingly contradictory discourses (critical pedagogy and postmodernism) remains a heated debate within critical pedagogy. On one side, the "critical/resistant postmodernists" incorporate postmodernism without giving up "possibility" as its ultimate objective. On the other side, other poststructuralists and postmodernists object to the very idea of possibility as "totalizing" and "moralizing."

The Contender: Feminism

Almost immediately after critical pedagogy emerged and its ideas were circulated, feminists (that is, white feminists) began to question and challenge critical pedagogy. Many feminists had already criticized earlier neo-Marxist theories and other critical theories, for their lack of attention to gender issues. What was new this time, though, was that feminists had gone beyond just criticizing the neglect of gender in critical pedagogy; they began to criticize critical pedagogy itself. Elizabeth Ellsworth, in her famous article "Why doesn't this feel empowering? Working through the repressive myths of critical pedagogy," challenges critical pedagogy head on, claiming that critical pedagogy, as it is, "perpetuates relations of domination" (Ellsworth, 1988/1992: 91). This is, according to Ellsworth, because the key assumptions underlying critical pedagogy are ahistorical and de-politicized abstractions. Ellsworth writes: "'[E]mpowerment', 'student voice', 'dialogue', and even the term 'critical' are repressive myths" (ibid.). For instance, she considers "student voice" as highly problematic, "because it is impossible to speak from all voices at once. Any individual woman's politicized voice will be partial, multiple, and contradictory" (ibid.: 104). Ellsworth thus argues that "student empowerment has been defined in the broadest possible humanistic terms, and becomes a 'capacity to act efficiently' in a way that fails to challenge any identifiable social or political position, institution, or group" (ibid.: 99).

Therefore, according to her, "dialogue," which critical pedagogy presents as a basis for democratic pedagogy, is "not only impossible but potentially repressive as well" (ibid.: 106).

In the same vein, Carmen Luke (1992) also problematizes the foundation of critical pedagogy. According to her, critical pedagogy is based on liberalism/modernism, which is a male-oriented theoretical construct. Luke argues that critical pedagogy is problematic because, "[i]n the discourse of critical pedagogy, the educational politics of emancipatory self- and social empowerment, and of emancipatory rationality and citizenship education, have been articulated in epistemic relation to liberal conceptions of equality and participatory democracy" (ibid.: 29). And these liberal conceptions, Luke further argues, construct "a masculinist subject which renders its emancipatory agenda for 'gender' theoretically and practically problematic" (ibid.: 25).

Based on these critiques, some feminists have presented "feminist poststructuralist theories" as a better direction for critical pedagogy (Luke & Gore, 1992). Why have they gravitated toward poststructuralism? The main reason is, as mentioned above, poststructuralism's focus on multiplicity and subject/identity. Feminists had been in need of new theories to express their frustration with the class-centrality of neo-Marxism. True, neo-Marxists have already gone beyond a class-only framework by accepting the co-centrality of power dynamics. For instance, Apple always sticks to the trinity—class, race, and gender. However, it could be that, even though neo-Marxists and other critical theorists have included gender and race in their discourse, feminists might have felt (and rightly so) that gender and patriarchy have not been treated seriously enough. The emphasis on multiplicity and the subject formation in poststructuralism is a right fit for feminists who have been looking to carve out space for their assertion. And at that time, poststructuralism provided the language to do so. In that sense, it seems logical that feminists have grabbed the post-theories (poststructuralism and postmodernism) in order to insert gender in the mix, with as much weight as class. Thus, Michel Foucault has become their favorite, competing against or dethroning the old symbol, Karl Marx.

The powerful insertion of poststructuralism into critical pedagogy is, no doubt, a great contribution by feminists. Yet, there are also some problems. It is not clear where critical pedagogy would go in the end if it rejects, as these feminists have proposed to do, basic conceptions that underlie critical theories, such as social justice, equality, and democracy. For instance, if we acknowledge that social justice is a modernist/liberal concept and thus to be abandoned, then what would and should be the guiding concepts for critical pedagogy? Or ought we not to search for guiding principles? If "it is gaps and ruptures in practice that offer the greatest insight and possibilities for change" (Orner, 1992: 84), then what kinds of gaps and ruptures offer the greatest insights, or are all ruptures equal insights and possibilities? How do gaps and ruptures offer possibilities for change? These are, indeed, very difficult and serious questions. While feminists have been successful in pioneering the introduction of poststructuralism and postmodernism into critical education theories, they have not been as successful in presenting alternatives to the modernist/liberal concepts that they have criticized.

Another issue is a lack of attention to race. There is no doubt that poststructural and postmodernist feminists have moved critical pedagogy from the singular to the plural, from class dominance to multiple marginalities. Yet, there are limitations to their own claims on pluralism regarding race. A good illustration of this limitation is Luke and Gore's book *Feminisms and Critical Pedagogy* (1992). Ellsworth's article (1988/1992) is about race, gender, and other marginalities, and in fact it is more about race than gender, as can be seen in the class she has based on this article: "Media and Anti-Racist Pedagogies." Yet, in Luke and Gore's book, race is absent, and Ellsworth's work is used for gender issues only. No author in Luke and Gore's book—nor any other who has responded to the book—seems to notice this very interesting silence on race. While the feminists have been right in challenging critical pedagogy to go beyond class by incorporating gender, they have not themselves been fully able to include other marginalities, particularly race. Thus, race has had to wait to enter into the discourse of critical pedagogy.

The Challenger: Race and Postcolonialism

Race is a thorny issue in the U.S., and has always been so. Neglect of race in critical theories has been raised and criticized for some time. But recently, race has become a particularly thorny issue within feminism. This is because feminist theories have, since the 1980s, pioneered new fronts in academic fields. As such, feminism naturally became a battleground for race and racism. For example, bell hooks (1984) gave a powerful criticism on white feminism. In her critique on the premise of the sisterhood/liberal and radical feminism, hooks does not subscribe to the common "innocent" explanations of white feminism, which posit an early lack of awareness (white women just did not know about other non-white women), or point to the developing status of the discipline (understandable at the beginning of the feminism/feminist movement, though white women/feminism are becoming more aware of their "whiteness"); nor does she accept the eventual trickle-down explanation (feminism, though it has been white, will be beneficial to all women, eventually). Instead, bell hooks argues that, "it [white feminism] has helped to consolidate class society by giving camouflage to these internal contradictions" (ibid.: 20–21).

As already mentioned above, the lack of attention to race in critical pedagogy was pointed out early on by some feminists, including Ellsworth (1988/1992). Since then, many others have also pointed out that critical pedagogy does not adequately address the issue of race (hooks, 1994; Ladson-Billings, 1994; Kincheloe & Steinberg, 1998; Leonardo, 2002, 2004; Allen, 2004; Grande, 2004; Lynn, 2004; Parker & Stovale, 2004; Spring, 2007). But, as Ricky Lee Allen rightly argues, these criticisms "have gone unheeded and the class-based political foundations of critical pedagogy have remained intact" (Allen, 2004: 123). Zeus Leonardo shares the same sentiment: "the question of race has played a secondary role in the development of critical pedagogy" (Leonardo, 2004: 117). The reason for this, according to Leonardo, is because "Marxian influence has been so great, critical pedagogy began its ascendance as a critique or problematization of class relations" (ibid.). While many critical theorists and educators agree on the significance of race, the relationship between class and race has been a contentious topic, and has been hotly debated for some time.

Similar to feminism's entry into critical pedagogy with poststructuralism, race has also entered critical pedagogy with a specific theoretical slant. For the last two decades or so, issues and studies on race have been advanced by postcolonial theories. Poststructuralism opened up an inroad for race studies. To simplify to the core, poststructuralism is, in essence, a study of the relationship between power and knowledge. Recent race studies took poststructuralism in their theoretical frames, and inserted race and colonialism into the equation. Thus, postcolonialism is, in essence, a study of the relationship between *colonial* power and *colonial* knowledge (Loomba, 1998). Led by Edward Said, Homi Bhabha, and Gayatri Spivak, postcolonialism became a powerful field of study, opening up a new arena for race studies. Since then, various race studies have flourished, such as on whiteness, white privilege, critical race theory, cultural studies, and identity politics.

Because of its focus on knowledge, postcolonial studies gears heavily toward culture, discourse, and superstructure (as with postmodernism in general). We can see it in the fact that the three masters of postcoloniality (Said, Bhabha, and Spivak) are all literary theorists, which is by no means a coincidence. While postcolonial theories have introduced and guided critical studies to a much-needed deeper understanding of race, the lopsided focus of the culturalist approach has been criticized for neglecting the structural and materialist understanding of race. But again, culturalism is not an exclusive issue for postcolonial studies. Culturalism has been the dominant trend in academic theories, as well as in social politics, since the 1980s. Of course, race and postcoloniality are not (and should not be) merely cultural. However, because of this specificity of discourse field, race is often equated with culturalism in opposition to materialism/economism of class (more in Chapter 3).

The Boundary Issue

What I have described above is the historical context and the origin of critical pedagogy as a *field of study*, not critical

pedagogy as an *idea*. As stated earlier, the idea of critical pedagogy existed long before the emergence of critical pedagogy as
a field of study/theory in the 1980s, and there were numerous
educators who were practicing critical pedagogy long before
there was the term "critical pedagogy." Today, it is likely that
there are teachers doing exactly what critical pedagogy promotes,
but who have never heard of critical pedagogy.

This leads us to the question of critical pedagogy's boundaries. How do we decide which are critical pedagogy and which
are not? Who are critical pedagogues and who are not? In other
words, where are the boundaries of critical pedagogy? And
should there be boundaries? These are tricky questions. On the
one hand, there are people who define critical pedagogy very
broadly, encompassing anything opposed to the mainstream
education paradigm. In its broadest definition, critical pedagogy is understood as analogous to critical education theories.
On the other hand, there are those who tend to define it more
narrowly. For instance, for some people, critical pedagogy equals
Freirean pedagogy. One source of these different interpretations of critical pedagogy is in the word "pedagogy." If one
interprets pedagogy as acts in the classroom (teaching), then
critical pedagogy tends to focus on the micro-level (mostly on
how to teach). On the other, if one understands pedagogy in a
broad way as "all acts of cultural [re]production" (Zavarzadeh &
Morton, 1994: 6), then critical pedagogy would include not only
the micro-level (teaching in schools), but also the macro-level
analysis (beyond schools to larger society).

A pertinent issue related to this book is the boundary between
critical pedagogy and neo-Marxist education theories. Again, the
very identity of critical pedagogy (as the "language of possibility") was formulated as a reaction to neo-Marxist theories.

However, critical pedagogy's reactions to neo-Marxist theories have not simply been critique or rejection. The reactions have varied from critiques, to further elaborations, to rejections. In some respects, critical pedagogy has been about the elaboration and extension (thus, continuation) of earlier critical education theories, and in other ways it has been about differentiating itself from earlier Marxist theories. There are, however, substantial commonalities and overlaps between the two, as we will see in later chapters. Thus, it is possible for one to regard critical pedagogy and neo-Marxist theories as basically the same, and therefore make no demarcation between the two. Yet, there are some people who may see the two as separate approaches and emphasize the differences between them. Thus, who is identified as a critical pedagogue and how one defines what critical pedagogy is depends on one's view of this relationship between the earlier neo-Marxist theories and the later critical pedagogy. Although there are overlaps between the two approaches, this book differentiates critical pedagogy from earlier neo-Marxist education theories, in order to capture the shifts that occurred within the field of critical education. Regardless of where one sees the boundaries of critical pedagogy to be, there have been some crucial changes in critical education, with the emergence of critical pedagogy. The search for a "language of possibility" and the influence of postmodernism has significantly moved the field of critical education in different directions.

3

THE THEORETICAL CONTEXT
Culture and Cultural Politics

Introduction

The emergence of critical pedagogy in the 1980s can be understood, fundamentally, as a new emphasis on culture. As an escape from economic determinism and aporia of neo-Marxist theories, critical pedagogy moved away from the economy toward culture. Critical pedagogy shifted its theoretical focus from the economic base (the unity of the productive forces and the relations of production) to the superstructure (particular historical belief, religious, juridical, political, or other systems). In fact, the very identity of critical pedagogy is centered around culture/cultural politics, thus differentiating and distancing it from the earlier critical theories of education. A clear indication of the cultural base of critical pedagogy can be found in the very definition of critical pedagogy. For instance, McLaren defines critical pedagogy "as a form of *cultural politics* that is fundamentally concerned with student[s'] experience" (McLaren, 1995: 42, emphasis added). Darder, Baltodanto, and Torres also argue that "critical pedagogy seeks to address the concept of *cultural politics* by both legitimating and challenging students' experiences and perceptions" (Darder et al., 2003: 11, emphasis added).

In "Critical pedagogy: A look at the major concepts" (2003), McLaren presents the following key concepts in critical pedagogy:

- forms of knowledge
- class
- culture
- dominant culture, subordinate culture, and subculture
- cultural forms
- hegemony
- ideology
- prejudice
- discourse
- hidden curriculum
- curriculum as a form of cultural politics, and
- cultural capital.

Evidently, the majority of these key concepts emphasize the sphere of culture and the superstructure, and show the predominance of cultural politics in critical pedagogy. The cultural base of critical pedagogy is also evidenced in its research methodologies. There is a strong inclination/gravitation toward ethnographic and anthropological studies. Qualitative studies—

such as interviews, life histories, case studies, and autobiographic ethnographies—are dominant and authoritative in critical pedagogy. Furthermore, culture has become not only the privileged site of epistemological standpoint, but also a site of political resistance and emancipatory politics. Now, cultural/ discourse analysis and deconstruction becomes the site for resistance and challenge to the system (more elaborated in Chapter 4).

That said, it has to be noted that the emphasis of culture is not limited to critical pedagogy. In recent years, cultural theories have also had significant influence on critical educational theories. Since the 1980s, we have witnessed an outpouring of education literature from cultural theories and cultural studies. For instance, the revived interest in multicultural education in recent years can be understood as the effect, or at least a signal, of the discovery and dominance of culture in educational discourses. Furthermore, this phenomenon is not limited to the field of education. During the last three decades, "culture" has become dominant, more generally, in the social sciences and the humanities, and has been widely used in cultural theories, cultural studies, cultural power, cultural resistance, and cultural politics. Moreover, cultural politics has become a dominant political position in the new social movements (Teodori, 1969; Harvey, 1990; Sanbonmatsu, 2004). It is, Michael Denning (2004) says, as if we have newly discovered culture, realizing suddenly that culture is everywhere, and that it is culture that really matters. This trend of cultural dominance is also not limited to the industrialized West. Although there are some differences and incompatibilities, cultural studies and cultural politics have become a global phenomenon within the last two decades.

Why has culture come to the forefront of critical pedagogy, as well as other academic studies and Left politics? Why has culture become so important? What are the political and economic contexts that have catalyzed this sudden move toward culture? What problems do the cultural theories address that were not addressed before? These are the questions this chapter aims to address. In contemplating these questions, one could focus on purely theoretical differences among and between scholars and approaches. For instance, one could, as many have already done, delineate the differences between Marxism and the post-theories (poststructuralism, postmodernism, and post-colonialism) on how they conceptualize culture. Unlike this approach, however, this chapter examines the historical and social contexts that have provoked the emergence of culture. As such, this chapter sketches the topic of "culture" with broad (and sometimes crude) strokes, since the goal here is not to examine different theories or theorists of culture, but rather to capture the larger framework of how these different cultural discourses and politics posit themselves.

The Meaning of Culture Question

In the 1970s, a new and full-blown form of cultural study emerged. Since then, this "contemporary cultural study" has not only radically changed how culture is understood, but also has positioned culture at the center of social and philosophical theories. Cultural theorists argue that this new focus on and attention to culture followed (and was necessitated by) dramatic changes in society since the 1970s (or since World War II, according to Lyotard [1984]). In the postindustrial and postmodern society, they argue, culture necessarily is (and has to be) a critically important center (to some, *the* center).

Many agree that the social system has gone through some dramatic changes since the 1970s. However, what is not agreed upon is whether this change is a fundamental break, or a change in degree. It has been hotly debated whether the change since the 1970s has signaled a break from the previous social condition, or just a change within the system. In other words, this ongoing contention has been over, as Zeus Leonardo (in a personal communication) aptly points out, whether the "post" in postmodernity means "after" modernity, or "late" modernity. In this way, the question of culture is ultimately a question about the very nature of society itself. If the postmodern condition is a complete break from modernity, it means that the Marxist framework is no longer valid in analyzing society/capitalism and presenting an alternative (roughly, this is the postmodernists' position). However, if the postmodern condition is understood as a late stage of modernity/capitalism, then Marxism is still relevant in some fashion (roughly, this is the neo-Marxists' position). As such, it is no wonder that the culture question has not only divided, but also has fueled disputes between the neo-Marxists and the post-theorists. This chapter, perhaps ambitiously, attempts to shed some light on the question of culture in lieu of its meaning for understanding the nature of society.

My central argument in this chapter is that culture has become important in the course of the 20th century, because of *changes in capitalism itself*. As I endeavor to outline the historical contexts of changes in capitalism through which culture studies and cultural politics have evolved, my treatment of "culture" in this chapter is inevitably broader than that of the British Centre for Contemporary Cultural Studies, or postmodern cultural studies. I define the turn to culture more broadly, which is a move away from the material base to the superstructure in social theories. Thus, my examination of the move toward culture proceeds from the early 20th century—roughly since the 1930s, covering major cultural theories from Antonio Gramsci's import of the concept of hegemony in the 1920s–1930s (Gramsci, 1971), to the Frankfurt School's attention to popular culture and mass media in the 1940s–1960s (Benjamin, 1937/1978; Adorno, 1938/1978, 1962/1978, 1973; Marcuse, 1969, 1972), to Louis Althusser's affective theory of ideology and ideological state apparatus (Althusser, 1971), to the Birmingham cultural studies (Hoggart, 1957; Thompson, 1957, 1958; Hall, 1958, 1980; Williams, 1961, 1963), to the poststructuralist and the postmodernist theories' focus on culture and knowledge since the 1970s (Foucault, 1977, 1980; Lyotard, 1984; Baudrillard, 1994). To reiterate, my focus is not to give a detailed review of these diverse theories, but to demonstrate how the fundamental changes in political economy have changed the significance and meaning of culture, and how the changes in the mode of capitalism have pushed culture to the center stage both in critical theories and Leftist politics. In short, mine is a material analysis of cultural studies and cultural politics.

Working Class Consciousness and Hegemony

Inspired by the Russian Revolution, there was a surge of revolutionary struggles after World War I, which spread globally to Asia, Africa, and Latin America (Tilly, 2004). However, it was apparently clear by the 1930s that the proletarian revolutionary possibility in Europe was all but lost. Instead of joining the international workers' movement, the working class in Europe supported the nationalistic fascism that emerged between the two world wars. With that, European proletariats were successfully incorporated into the capitalist system (Arato & Gebhardt, 1978; Davis, 1999; Wallerstein, 2004a). Why did the proletariats acquiesce to the capitalist system whose foundation was built on exploitation of their own labor? In other words, why would the working class accept going against its own class interests? It is this very problem that became a central question to Marxists in the early part of the 20th century. Subsequently, this question directed Marxists' attention to the sphere of the superstructure (ideology and culture), on which Karl Marx and Friedrich Engels did not fully elaborate. Antonio Gramsci tried to answer this question with the cultural-political hegemony of the bourgeoisie, while György Lukács focused on the ideological crisis of the proletariat.

Recalling Marx, the dominant ideology of a society is the ideology of the dominant class, and the working class buys into the dominant ideology mainly on account of their false consciousness. To put it simply, the working class fails to see their own interests because they are duped, and they are duped because the ruling class dominates the very means of production of ideology. However, unlike this rather crude explanation provided by Marx, Gramsci (1971) saw the process not solely as a matter of falsity, but rather a matter of concession and compromise. For Gramsci, the crucial questions were: Why did Mussolini's fascism rise in Italy? Why did the Italian people support it? And how could the working class gain power in bourgeois-dominated Europe? Gramsci saw the Italian people, including the working class, as having consented to and accepted fascism, rather than having been forced or duped, because the ruling bloc was able to establish hegemony. In this hegemony-building process, Gramsci realized the crucial role the intellectuals played. According to Gramsci, it was the "traditional intellectuals" who developed, articulated, and legitimated the ideology of the dominant class. As such, in order to counter this hegemony, he argued, the working class needed its own intellectuals (he called them the "organic intellectuals") who would formulate counter-hegemonic ideologies. Thus, for Gramsci, the class war was waged not only over the state power ("war of maneuver"), but also on the level of ideology and consciousness ("war of position"). Hence, Gramsci proclaimed that the superstructure is as important as, if not more important than, the material base.

Lukács (1923/1971) also rejected the false consciousness thesis. Like Gramsci, he highlighted the importance of cultural mediation in the formation of working class consciousness. First of all, Lukács emphasized the complexity of cultural mediation. He rejected the view that culture and literary representation automatically correspond with class interests. On the one hand, cultural representation could be emancipatory, if it presented the vantage point of proletariats by signifying the totality of social order. On the other hand, cultural representation could be a form of "reification," if it fragmented and dislocated our reality and experiences. With increasing commodification of cultural representations, Lukács argued that culture became more of a form of reification than of emancipation, and thus functioned as a controlling mechanism for ensuring the passivity of the working classes (Smith, 2000). This theme was later picked up and further developed by others, particularly the Frankfurt School.

Through Gramsci and Lukács, ideology and culture were given a far greater importance than before, thus emerging as crucial spheres to be closely analyzed in understanding the con-sciousness of the working class (Sparks, 1996). Later, when the Birmingham cultural studies tried to explain why the British working class supported Margaret Thatcher (basically the same question as Gramsci's one of why the Italian working class supported Mussolini), it is Gramsci that the Birmingham Centre revived, and from which they developed the hegemony theory of culture (ibid.). Just like their British counterpart, the American working class also helped the rise of the Reagan administration in the early 1980s. Perhaps this similarity in political situations is one of the reasons why British cultural studies have deeply influenced the intellectual and political Left of the U.S.

Mass Culture Industry and the Subject

As Gramsci tried to understand the rise of fascism in Italy, the Frankfurt School attempted to explain the rise of fascism in Germany. How did the civilized German people, who inherited rich intellectual traditions, support Hitler's fascism and commit such inhumane and unimaginable atrocities against other human beings? According to the Frankfurt critical theorists, the answer can be found in the emergence of mass communi-cation and the culture industry, and its impacts on culture and social subjects. The Frankfurt School stressed that the emergence of a mass culture industry changed the function that art and culture had played in society. Since the Enlightenment period, art, a realm of the life-world, was considered against and beyond the system-world, which was dominated by rationality (Arato, 1978). Art used to be poised as an antidote against the destruc-tive instrumental rationality of capitalism, and against the effects of functionalism (Harvey, 1990). Particularly, the rise of popular culture was considered as a progressive force, challenging the elite/bourgeois culture. By insisting that cultural representations of everyday people were also art, the emergence of popular culture challenged the idea that only elite culture is worthy of embodying artistic values. Art and culture were no longer a monopoly of the aristocrats.

However, with the emergence of mass media and the culture industry, the progressive force of popular culture was severely diminished. It is this new development of mass media and the commercial production of mass culture to which the Frankfurt critical theory paid close attention. According to the Frankfurt School, mass media and the culture industry transformed popular culture into commercialized mass culture. Just like other manufacturing goods, culture had now become mass produced, packaged, and distributed as consumer goods. In other words, art and culture underwent what Andrew Arato (1978) has termed "thingfication." This change was crucial, according to the Frankfurt School, because it explained why working class culture and consciousness could no longer be independent of their own class interest. As subjects and consciousness were now constructed by mass commercial culture, the close relation between class and culture/consciousness was fundamentally broken. As a result, the Frankfurt School contended that popular culture no longer represented the culture of people. Instead, culture became a major mechanism of social control. This is how the Frankfurt School explained the lack of working class consciousness, and their acceptance of Nazism, as they carried on media studies in the U.S. during the Nazi period (see Jay, 1973).

The study of mass media by the Frankfurt School led to a new question of how mass media and the culture industry impact the formation of "the subject." Among others, the work

of Louis Althusser is significant on the topic of subject formation. His theory laid the foundation for contemporary accounts
of cultural identity and the subject. Althusser attempted to
overcome the failures of Marxist economic analysis, in order
to properly explain the role of ideology (culture being a sub-part
of ideology) in the reproduction of the relations of production.
The complex and sometimes contradictory relations within the
superstructure (this is "articulation," not "mediation"—a point
to which I will return later) defy the previous notion of the
subject as a passive agent determined by class interests. Althusser
(1971) contended that the ideological state apparatuses (such
as the family, education system, political parties, trade unions,
religious organizations, mass media, and cultural agents) played
a significant role in the formulation of the subject. The basic
point of Althusser with regard to the role of ideological state
apparatuses (ISAs) is that superstructural institutions have
become much more complex, and their role and influence
have increased, with growing intervention in the 20th century
(see Smith, 2000). Althusser's identification of ideology as a
representation of the "imaginary" relationship of individuals to
their material conditions, and the subjectification or the creation
of subjects through discourse and interpellation became the basis
of much of the later cultural studies (see Leonardo, 2003b).

As most Frankfurt School scholars were Jews who were exiled
from Germany, it is quite understandable that their account of
culture is quite grim, and their prospect for social change is quite
pessimistic. Critical theory in general has become increasingly
nihilistic from the late 1950s onward. The subject basically
disappears and the society becomes all-powerful (Piccone,
1978). As such, it is hard, if not impossible, to hold onto the
existence of an autonomous subject. This means the very idea of

the free and autonomous subject is rendered hopeless, because of the tight grip of the present Western system on the consciousness not only of the dominant, but also of the dominated (this theme is later echoed in Freire, 1970/1997). With the death of the subject or the arrival of posthumanism (Hardt & Negri, 2000), obviously it is hard to even imagine the possibility for radical social change. This theme is carried on prominently in the later development of poststructuralism and postmodernism. For instance, we see a similar description of power as disciplining subjects in the totally administered society described by Michel Foucault (1977).

State Capitalism and the Remaking of the Working Class

Above, I described how superstructure, ideology, and mass culture have emerged as significant themes in critical theories, and how cultural theories have evolved to focus on subject formation through the mass media, the educational system, and the prisons, as studied by the Frankfurt School, Althusser, and, later, Foucault. This growing attention to culture is a result of the class war that is now waged through cultural interventions by the cultural industries and "state cultural apparatuses" (Denning, 2004: 161). In order to better understand how culture has come to be a site of class struggle, we need to examine the change in the mode of capital accumulation in the first part of the 20th century.

In the early 20th century, capitalism in the industrialized West plunged into a severe crisis. With this crisis, it was recognized that the market could not regulate itself (this is the end of laissez-faire/liberal capitalism), and thus the state had to intervene and regulate the market in order to stabilize the economy (this is the beginning of state capitalism). The emergence of totalitarian regimes in the 1930s and 1940s—not only fascism in Germany, Italy, and Japan, but also Stalinism in the USSR and the New Deal in the U.S.—was due to this major crisis in capitalism (Pollock, 1941/1978; Arato, 1978; Harvey 1990; Wallerstein, 2004a). In fact, Friedrich Pollock (1941/1978)—a Frankfurt School-affiliated scholar—argued that Nazism was partly a response to the crisis of liberal capitalism and that Nazism was considered as a necessary political form for a stabilized monopoly of capitalism. This change from liberal capitalism to state capitalism has a significant meaning for culture. The state regulation of capitalist economies and the increased role of the state within capitalism increased the importance of the political-administrative sphere. As the axis moved from economy to politics, the sphere of culture became increasingly crucial for social reproduction and legitimation (Arato, 1978).

After the savage depression and the near collapse of capitalism in the 1930s, a new mode of capitalism was devised. The understanding was that the crisis of liberal capitalism was due to the falling consumption of manufacturing goods that were produced in vast quantities. The underlying motive of Fordism (the five-dollar, eight-hour work day) was to solve this over-production and underconsumption problem. Fordism provided enough income to workers to purchase the consumer products, driving up consumptive practices, which in turn increased production. With more income and leisure time (due to shorter working hours), workers were transformed into the much-needed consumers. After several different experiments, Fordism rose as the dominant configuration after World War II in the U.S. The long economic boom era from 1945 to 1973 was built on this combination of Fordist-Keynesianism (Harvey, 1990).

Post-war Fordism and the economic boom in the West had significant impacts on class structure and working class culture. With the expanded opportunity for higher education (particularly due to the GI bill), increased residency in the new suburbs, and the increased power of mass consumption, the working class was transformed and remade during this period. The middle class lifestyle was comfortably adopted by the working class. This embourgeoisement of the working class inevitably altered the working class culture and the formation of their class consciousness. For instance, Stanley Aronowitz (1989) demonstrates how the development of the suburbs in the post-war U.S. broke down the working class community and fractured working class culture. It is no coincidence that around this time working class representation largely disappeared from the mass media as well. Up until the early 1960s, the representation of the working class (that is, white workers) was, though small in numbers, present in films and television. But from the mid-1970s, media representation of workers had basically disappeared. Thus, Aronowitz argues, working class children today have a harder time in forging a class identity, because "they confront a media complex that consistently denies their existence, or displaces working-class male identity to other, upwardly mobile occupations, for example, police work, football players, and other sites where conventional masculine roles are ubiquitous" (Aronowitz, 1989: 204).

The remaking of the working class and the transformation of working class culture further widened the gap between one's class position and one's class consciousness. The independent making of the working class culture seemed no longer feasible, not just because of the mass cultural industry, but also because the working class itself had changed. It is in this historical context that British cultural studies emerged in the 1960s, and this is why the Centre for Cultural Studies focused on the culturalist research agenda of studying working class culture and education, beginning with E.P. Thompson and Richard Hoggart (see Sparks, 1996; Smith, 2000).

The Cultural Turn and Contemporary Cultural Studies

As stated above, culture (as a part of the superstructure) has become increasingly more significant in critical theories since the early 20th century. However, there was a crucial break in cultural theories in the late 1960s and 1970s, which is often called the "cultural turn." This was the beginning of "contemporary cultural studies," and with that, a whole host of neo-Marxist and post-Marxist theories have emerged: from Althusser, to the Birmingham cultural studies, to the poststructuralist and postmodernist theories, to the postcolonial theories. It is neither possible nor my intention to review these diverse cultural theories. Instead, I will delineate four closely related characteristics of contemporary cultural studies, especially highlighting how they differ from earlier approaches to culture.

The first characteristic of contemporary cultural studies is about how culture is to be understood. While earlier Marxist or neo-Marxist theories paid increasing attention to the sphere of superstructure and culture, they still maintained a close relationship between culture and the economic base, ultimately in the form of the latter determining the former. In contrast, contemporary cultural studies basically abandons the centrality of the material base in its discourse, and argues that culture bears no concrete relation to the material base, or at least is autonomous of it (e.g., Hindess & Hirst 1977; Laclau & Mouffe, 1984). As such, poststructuralists and postmodernists understand culture (e.g., language and representation) to be free-floating, fractured, indeterminate, and infinitive—detached from any basis/base that can be traced to social structures and relations. This is made possible by a particular reading of Gramsci through the concept of "articulation," which suggests the conjuncture of events that arbitrarily congeal and are in no way determined by the economy.

This new view on culture as an autonomous sphere is, I think, due to changes in social reality. With the global saturation of mass media and communication, it is more widely recognized and acclaimed that the reality of our time is a reality/image constructed and represented via mass media. Culture and signs now create our reality, as portrayed poignantly (and somewhat dreadfully) by Jean Baudrillard (1994) in his simulation theory (see also Leonardo, 2003a). Representation is now our reality, and, as Baudrillard and others argue, there is no such thing as "reality" outside of representation. Our experience is of a simulation of reality rather than reality itself (thus, Baudrillard calls it a "simulacrum"), a chimerical relation with the real. In short, culture has graduated to the status of reality (Denning, 2004).

Second, as contemporary cultural studies see culture as having much more autonomy than before, they place a greater degree of importance on culture. In contemporary cultural studies, the role of culture (along with education) has expanded and become much more significant in explaining the reproduction of capitalism as a system. The contemporary culturalists do not see culture as subservient or subordinate to the economy.

Hence, Althusser's famous turn to reproduction and away from relations of production has signaled the new concern with the ideological process of capitalism. In fact, Althusser's concept of "overdeterminism" allows the superstructure to affect the base, cultural life rebounding in an unpredictable way onto economic life. As such, these theorists place a greater emphasis upon the role of political and ideological strategies, through which hegemonic projects are to be constructed. A major reason for this shift is because culture itself has become an important part of the economic realm. The production and consumption of culture has become a core industry in global capitalism. The mass media, advertising, production, and distribution of knowledge, information, and communication have become the leading sector of economy within industrialized societies, replacing the prominence of the manufacturing industry, once a leading sector of capitalism (thus, the "postindustrial" society). This is precisely the theme that Jean-François Lyotard (1984) explored in his seminal book, *The Postmodern Condition*. According to Lyotard, the postmodern condition has to be understood in the cultural field and no longer within relations or modes of production.

The third characteristic of contemporary cultural studies is that they reject the idea that cultural representation is a simple manifestation of class interest. In the new cultural theories, the identity/subject formation is understood as a much looser and more complex process neither deterministic nor teleological (undetermined, and unexpected/unintended). Cultural representation and interpretation is viewed as more of a negotiation of meanings and "articulations," rather than as a "mediation" of class interests or the underlying economic foundation

(Smith, 2000). This means we are seeing different models of social formation. As seen, for instance, in Althusser, "[t]he centre of attention shifted from the relations between base and superstructure into an elaboration of the internal articulation of the superstructure itself" (Sparks, 1996: 82). From there, it is not difficult to see why symbols, representations, and meanings have become a major focus in contemporary cultural studies. With that, the focus of investigation has also shifted from the production of culture toward the consumption of culture. As it has been realized that culture plays more of an influential role in identity formation, popular culture has emerged as a key topic in contemporary cultural studies.

And finally, given that cultural process and identity formation are now understood as more complex and loose, it is acknowledged that identity is not necessarily constructed according to class position and interest. Instead, other forms of social antagonism—race, gender, sexuality, for instance—are as relevant as class to identity formation and to the social formation. The thesis of the omnipresent centrality of class is severely tested and challenged. Here, as we know, there have been hotly contested debates on the relationships between class, race, and gender among Marxists, feminists, and anti-race theorists. A core assertion of contemporary cultural studies is that we should go beyond the class-dominance of critical theories, and acknowledge the co-centrality of gender, race, and other forms of social marginality with class. Consequently, since the 1970s, we see the rise of the new social movements, mainly based on identity politics, such as the civil rights movements and the women's movement, followed by the gay and lesbian rights movement, green movements, and multicultural and anti-race movements (Harvey, 1990; Sanbonmatsu, 2004; Tilly, 2004).

Postmodernism

To understand the new cultural politics, we need first to grasp what postmodernism is and how it has emerged. Postmodernism has two counterparts—modernism and Marxism. First, postmodernism is a reflection of a critical and shaken awareness concerning modernity and modern projects of the West (Lyotard, 1984; Harvey, 1990). While the 20th century has brought remarkable advances in inventions and technological breakthroughs, it has also witnessed tremendous disasters and tragic inhumanities. Two world wars, fascism, and the Holocaust have shattered the faith in the Enlightenment project of modernism. Here, we need to reminded that, as W.E.B. Du Bois (1947/1975) has pointed out, there is no Nazi-like atrocity that the Christian civilization of Europe has not long been practicing against the colonized bodies in all parts of world. However, it is the Holocaust that shook European sensibility (see Césaire, 1955/2000). In addition, the 20th century has created colonial wars, atrocities, genocides, and nuclear arms (enough to kill all human beings several hundred times over). As such, postmodernism rejects, or at least casts doubts on, the Enlightenment philosophy of modernism.

On the other hand, postmodernism is also a critique of, or an incredulity toward Marxism. The rise of Stalinism during the 1920s and 1930s had already created doubts among the Western Left who, in one way or another, had looked at the Soviet Union as a great historical alternative to the capitalist West (in fact, the Frankfurt School was internally divided regarding the Soviet question). However, following the Soviet invasion of Hungary in 1956 and the forceful intervention in the 1968 Prague Spring of Czechoslovakia, it had become clear to many Western Leftists that the Soviet project had failed. Disillusioned, the New Left began to see socialist theory as in need of serious revision, or complete abandonment. As such, postmodernism no longer believes in "salvation," neither of the spirit (modernism), nor of the revolution (Marxism), thus forging, as Lyotard puts it, "incredulity toward metanarratives" (Lyotard, 1984: xxiv). It is within this context of a skeptical stance toward systemic changes and political struggles that we have to understand why the only salvation for Theodor Adorno (1938/1978) was the arts (he once aspired to be a professional violinist), why Michel Foucault (1988) endeavored on "the care of self" (he goes back to ancient Greece for this), and why Peter Sloterdijk (1997) presented "kynicism" (the cheekiness of body functions) as an alternative against cynical reason.

The collapse of the Soviet project and the frustration with the Enlightenment projects of modernity has marked the beginning of new critical theories and new political praxes (thus, the "New Left"). The old class-based social movements have been replaced with new social movements. Instead of focusing on capitalism or the state, a new cohort of critical theorists after 1968 has looked into new spheres (see Brennan, 2006). No longer believing that changing the system (e.g., social and political institutions) would bring genuine transformation and human liberation, the New Left has turned to the body/individual/local struggles as alternatives. This is why, in the last three decades, we have seen the rise of identity politics (the civil rights movement, the women's movement, the gay movement), localized/grassroots politics ("think globally, act locally"), and personal politics ("personal is political").

In short, postmodernism has instituted culture as a privileged site for resistance and emancipatory politics. From this impetus, multifaceted cultural politics have emerged over the last few decades. And the meanings of culture and cultural politics are diverse. There are various dimensions to what is meant by cultural politics: culture as life-world against instrumental reason; cultural politics as popular culture against elite/ institution culture; cultural politics as civil society against the state; and cultural politics as multiculturalism and subaltern/ postcolonial project against Eurocentrism. However, an underlying commonality among these various cultural politics is the idea that, ultimately, politics has turned to culture, or culture has become an important site for politics. In other words, the postmodern condition now has to be understood within the context of the cultural field, and no longer within relations of production (Baudrillard, 1975, 1994; Lyotard, 1984). For this reason, it is within this cultural field that the counter-hegemonic war must be waged and where possibilities are to be found again. While earlier/old social movements focused on the economy, the new social movements now focus on culture. As such, knowledge, images, representation, and identity are now understood as important as, if not more important than, strikes, wages, and working conditions.

Cultural Studies in Education

So far in this chapter, I have attempted to answer the question of why culture has moved to the forefront of critical theories and the politics of the 20th century in the West. I have tried to make a case—perhaps in a somewhat functionalistic way—that the rise of cultural studies and cultural politics is due to the transition from the modern society of the 18th and 19th centuries to the postindustrial society of the 20th century. While the transition to

Fordist-Keynesian capitalism in the 1940s has brought culture and superstructure more clearly into the picture, the transition to postindustrial society in the 1970s has brought what we now know as full-fledged cultural studies and cultural politics.

As stated at the beginning of this chapter, culture has become an important topic in critical education literature during the past three decades. Various cultural theories have influenced cultural studies in education, and there are diverse meanings and uses of culture in the educational literature. It is beyond the scope of this chapter to review the extensive literature on the disparate cultural theories in education. Instead, I will briefly lay out how cultural politics are conceptualized and utilized in critical educational literature by teasing out multiple layers of different levels/dimensions. By utilizing and modifying Michael Denning's work (2004), I will identify five cultural theories in critical education theories: (1) hegemonic theory of culture, (2) commodity theory of culture, (3) resistance theory of culture, (4) disciplinary theory of culture, and (5) identity/postcolonial theory of culture.

Initiated by the influential work of Bowles and Gintis (1976), critical education theorists in the 1970s and early 1980s have attempted to explain the mechanisms whereby the school (re)produces the hierarchical economic system. In this attempt, they have been heavily influenced by the *hegemonic theory of culture* from the British cultural studies that have come to the attention of U.S. academics of that era. These critical educational theorists have employed Gramsci, Althusser, and Stuart Hall, and have advanced concepts, such as hidden curriculum, ideology/hegemony, and schools as a state apparatus (Apple, 1979, 1982; Dale et al., 1981; Giroux, 1983, 1988b; Carnoy & Levin, 1985). The main claim of these works is that the school, as a part of culture/superstructure, plays a significant role in (re)producing and legitimating the hegemony of capitalist society. Schools and education accomplish this through diverse mechanisms —by certain knowledge they choose to include or exclude in the curriculum, by the norms and values they convey to students, and by the social interactions and practices they utilize to sort out students for future careers. Ideology critique is the core of this hegemonic theory of culture, which is arguably still the dominant approach in cultural studies of education today.

The *commodity theory of culture* by Pierre Bourdieu has also made a significant impact on cultural studies in education. Bourdieu has approached culture as a commodity form, and has analyzed how culture has emerged as an investment in the creation of cultural capital (Bourdieu & Passeron, 1977). As a result of the commodification of culture, culture (that is, elite culture as capital) now becomes an important mechanism to create "distinction" (Bourdieu, 1984). Bourdieu's concepts —such as habitus, cultural capital, symbolic violence, and distinctions—have provided powerful tools in revealing the power relations embedded in school knowledges. For instance, Bourdieu has exposed the asymmetry of power through critique of how certain knowledges are considered as high-status, while others are seen as low-status. The concept of "cultural capital," in particular, has been widely utilized in analyzing not only class, but also race and gender power dynamics in school knowledge (e.g., Lareau, 1989; Delpit, 1995; Reay, 1998; Harry & Klingner, 2006; Paik & Walberg, 2007).

Paul Willis' (1977) *Learning to Labor* is significant in that his work has highlighted the loose yet active nature of culture. Unlike the hegemony and the commodity theory of culture, Willis has described cultural reproduction less as a seamless process, but, rather, a loose one with a contradictory mixture of penetration, rationality, distortion, and final incorporation. What Willis has highlighted is that, first, culture inherently has points of weakness involved with contradiction and resistance, and, second, culture maintains relative autonomy due to the effects of relatively autonomous meanings, such as those found in sexism and racism. Contrary to the deterministic and gloomy depiction of the role of education in hegemony and commodity theories, the resistance theory of Willis has provided some potentiality for changes and possibility. Thus, it is not hard to understand why this *resistance theory of culture* has been appreciatively embraced by critical educators. A series of studies has followed, examining the resistance dynamics of culture and exploring culture as a site for resistance, struggles, and changes (e.g., Apple, 1982; Giroux, 1983; Weis, 1990; MacLeod, 1995; Kenny, 2000).

Another theory that has impacted critical education literature is the *disciplinary theory of culture* by Foucault. Unlike the commodity theory, Foucault's theory conceptualizes culture as dispersed systems of surveillance and the disciplining of desire by the state and quasi-state institutions, such as prisons, armies, hospitals, and schools (Foucault, 1977). In this scheme, schools are a powerful surveillance agency, disciplining the body and formulating the subjectivities of students. The effects of power in Foucault are all-encompassing and omnipresent, which is, in fact, a very pessimistic view. Foucault's theory of culture, however, is utilized in sometimes conflicting ways in critical education. Some employ Foucault's concept of disciplinary power to expose schools as a system of surveillance, while others highlight more the rupture or fracture of the power mechanism to envision schools as a site of possibility for resistance and change (e.g., Aronowitz, & Giroux, 1991; Giroux, 1991; Popkewitz & Brennan, 1997; Marshall, 1998; Popkewitz & Fendler, 1999; Palermo, 2002; Bratich et al., 2003; Gabbard, 2006; Peters & Besley, 2007). Particularly, feminist education literature has been heavily influenced by Foucault's conception of power/ knowledge in the past two decades (e.g., Lather, 1991; Luke & Gore, 1992; Gore, 1993; St. Pierre & Pillow, 2000). For one, Foucault's idea of "subjugated knowledge" (Foucault, 1980) is taken up by feminists and race theorists who have been challenging class-dominated theories of culture.

The *identity/postcolonial theory of culture* is another approach that has become visible only recently in cultural studies in education. In this approach, culture is conceptualized mainly as communities of people, due to the influence of Stuart Hall's focus on the national-popular, and to the place of racisms in its formation (Denning, 2004). Now, cultural theories increasingly are about how culture produces people—nation, race, immigrant, diaspora, and postcolonial subject—with the aim to critically examine and to challenge Eurocentrism. Yet, this identity/postcolonial theory of culture goes beyond the scope of multiculturalism, in that "the culture of the subaltern is a product of a dialectic of self and other, where the self is objectified as the other and denied any reciprocity of recognition" (ibid.: 90). Critical education literature is deeply influenced by this identity/postcolonial theory of culture. We have recently seen revived interest in multiculturalism and a plethora of cultural studies employing postcolonial/subaltern theories in critical education literature (e.g., Giroux, 1995; McLaren, 1997; McCarthy, 1998; Leonardo, 2002, 2004, 2005; Allen, 2004; Darder & Torres, 2004; Grande, 2004; Apple & Buras, 2006; Buras & Motter, 2006).

Culture in Critical Pedagogy

As mentioned at the beginning of the chapter, culture is positioned at the center of critical pedagogy. However, the realization of the significance of culture and the superstructure is not new. Influenced by neo-Marxism (Antonio Gramsci, Louis Althusser, and Raymond Williams), the educational Left had already examined the importance of culture, hegemony, and the state in the decades prior to the emergence of critical pedagogy as a disciplinary field (Willis, 1977; Apple, 1979, 1982; Dale et al., 1981; Carnoy & Levin, 1985). What was new in critical pedagogy, then, was the *way* culture was to be understood. Unlike previous neo-Marxist cultural theories, the new version of cultural studies in critical pedagogy was heavily influenced by poststructuralism and postmodernism. In other words, while we see all five approaches to culture in critical pedagogy, the most dominant cultural theories in critical pedagogy are the disciplinary theory of culture and identity/postcolonial theory of culture.

This transition to poststructural culturalism in critical pedagogy has been a serious point of contention between neo-Marxists and post-theorists. For instance, McLaren argues that postmodern culturalism is the main reason why critical pedagogy can no longer provide a viable alternative for social change. According to McLaren, "critical pedagogy has become so completely psychologized, so liberally humanized, so technologized, and so conceptually postmodernized, that its current relationship to broader liberation struggles seems severely attenuated if not fatally terminated" (McLaren, 1998: 448). I agree with McLaren that the "ludic postmodernism" (Ebert, 1996) contributed to the culturalization of critical pedagogy.

However, I do not think that this "infatuation of post-modernism" of critical pedagogues is as strong as McLaren and some others have characterized. Perhaps it is because the post-modernist "language" is not readily accessible to many ordinary educators. More importantly, I think the overall project of social change and possibility in critical pedagogy does not mesh well with postmodernist positions. Moreover, I think that the American sensibility is too optimistic, pragmatic, and moralistic to be genuinely "ludic," which is more of a Parisian chic. I see postmodernism not as a cause, but rather as a reflection of, or a reaction to, the legitimization crisis of the Western welfare states (Habermas, 1975) and the crisis of the imperial global capitalism (Amin, 1997; Hardt & Negri, 2000).

In closing, I will briefly address some concerns related to culturalism and cultural politics in critical pedagogy. First, the approach to culture in critical pedagogy is very diverse, complex, and sometimes confusing. At one end of the spectrum, culture is viewed as a medium of discipline and social control, while, at the other end, culture is viewed as a site of resistance and possibility. Overall, I think the current use of culture in critical pedagogy sways more toward the resistance/possibility end of the spectrum. By magnifying the contradictory nature of culture, however, these studies tend to glorify the power of culture in transforming society. This is partly due to their attempt to overcome the seemingly pessimistic position of earlier Marxist theories of education. In a way, culture is utilized to rescue the critical theories of education from a presumably no-solution alternative. Yet, I think it is somewhat dangerous to become too enamored by talks of resistance. Over-resistance and over-contradiction is not the same as the crumbling of the social system.

Second, while cultural spheres are no doubt important in counter-hegemonic struggles, the problem with these cultural politics is that they overestimate the power of cultural struggles and neglect the material structures of society (Ahmad, 1995; Bourne, 1999). This "culturalism" of critical pedagogy has already been challenged and criticized (McLaren 1998; Apple, 2000; Scatamburlo-D'Annibale & McLaren, 2004). For instance, Michael Apple argues,

> [s]ome of it [critical pedagogy] is disconnected from the gritty materialities of daily economic, political, cultural, and educational struggles. Some of it *does* romanticize the cultural at the expense of equally powerful traditions of analysis based in political economy and the state. And some of it *does* place so much emphasis on "post" that it forgets the structural realities that set limits on real people in real institutions in everyday life.
>
> (Apple, 2000: 253, original emphasis)

In doing so, Scatamburlo-D'Annibale and McLaren contend that "culturalist arguments are deeply problematic both in terms of their penchant for de-emphasizing the totalizing (yes totalizing!) power and function of capital and for their attempts to employ culture as a construct that would diminish the centrality of class" (Scatamburlo-D'Annibale & McLaren, 2004: 185). As such, it has been pointed out that cultural politics neither address nor provide a solution to major "structural" issues of inequality that dominate the educational system and society. Jenny Bourne captures this problem succinctly:

> [I]n throwing out the bath water of "economic determinism" and "class reductionism", [poststructuralism and deconstruction] had thrown out the baby of political struggle against capital and the state.

In its stead, there was now a "cultural politics" which challenged "social blocs" in civil society.

(Bourne, 1999: 135)

Third, a basic political stance of postmodern cultural politics is "hostility toward totality," and in general, cultural politics bear some incredulity toward meta-narratives. In a sense, I think this is a progress in our awareness and sensibility. Acknowledgement of heterogeneity can be a sensible antidote against Eurocentrism, or Eurocentric universalism. Along with that, a keen recognition of difference and "otherness," which cultural politics promotes, advances democratic principles. However, cultural/postmodern politics can lead to fragmented and single issue-based praxis, which generally takes the form of anti-state strategies. The problem with anti-state strategies and celebration of differences may not be a proper position to fight against powerful global capitalism. Instead, as some critics warn, celebration of differences actually helps in deepening neoliberal global capitalism. Amin's critique is worth quoting here:

> The suggested anti-state strategy united perfectly with capital's strategy, which is busy "limiting public interventions" (deregulating) for its own benefit, reducing the role of the State to its police functions. In a similar way, the anti-nation discourse encourages the acceptance of the role of the U.S. as military superpower and world policeman.
>
> (Amin, 2004: 27)

In other words, capitalism is able to make certain accommodations to culture.

And finally, we need to be less sanguine and more cautious when applying cultural studies and cultural politics—especially, postmodern culturalism—to the realities of the majority of people in the Third World. It is true that globalization has brought homogenization around the globe. We see the globalization of popular culture: music, clothes, movies, and other popular media (one could call it "Californization" or "Hollywoodization" of global culture). Yet, globalization has also brought fragmentation and diversification (Castells, 1996; Castells et al., 1999; Hardt & Negri, 2000; Harvey, 2000; Amin, 2004). Heightened ethnic identity and intensified ethnic conflicts are just one example; the rise of fundamentalism (religious, as well as secular) is another example. Some parts of the globe— Africa in particular—are becoming more marginalized in the global network. Global capitalism has created more polarization, widening the gap between the rich and the poor countries. This is why postmodernism and cultural politics may not sit well with people in the South, where the brutalities of economic capitalism are still formidable forces. In other words, one senses that the cultural turn is a First World roundabout and crisis. Culturalism sounds more like a luxury for many people around the globe whose livelihoods are threatened by global capitalism. If cultural studies and cultural politics fail to adequately incorporate the gritty material reality of global capitalism, they could become merely a hollow intellectual exercise.

4

ALTERNATIVE PROJECTS OF CRITICAL PEDAGOGY

Introduction

Critical pedagogy is an attempt to find a "language of possibility," particularly against the neo-Marxist theories. While there are variations, neo-Marxist theories' conclusion, generally, is that schools (re)produce the inequalities of societies. Even the resistance theory of Paul Willis (1977) does not, in the end, go beyond the (re)production thesis. Then how has critical pedagogy overcome this seemingly pessimistic direction/conclusion of neo-Marxist education theories? What alternatives has critical pedagogy presented? This chapter aims to identify the main alternative projects presented by critical pedagogy.

Critical pedagogy is still an emerging field, and as such, it embodies several branches of ideas for alternatives. However, as reviewed in previous chapters, critical pedagogy has emerged under the heavy influence of poststructural and postmodernist theories. This context has shaped the identity and orientation of critical pedagogy, and this, in turn, has led critical pedagogy into certain directions in its quest for alternatives. So, while there are a wide variety of ideas within critical pedagogy, I think we can identify some dominant trends and approaches. This chapter focuses on these dominant approaches in critical pedagogy, which I call the "mainstream" critical pedagogy. First, this chapter introduces two main agendas of critical pedagogy—transformation of knowledge (curriculum) and pedagogy (in the narrow sense, i.e., teaching)—with a special focus on how, if at all, critical pedagogy differs from earlier neo-Marxist education theories. Second, the chapter identifies and critically examines dominant alternative projects that are presented by mainstream critical pedagogy.

Two Agendas of Critical Pedagogy

Critical pedagogy offers different approaches to different aspects of education, from curriculum, instruction, and evaluation, to classroom management. And its ideas are significantly different from—and are often opposed to—the mainstream education paradigm. These differences are due to its core concepts, which constitute the foundations of critical pedagogy, and from which critical pedagogy builds its own ideas/theories/ practices of education. The fundamental core themes of critical pedagogy include:

1. education as a change agent (Freire, 1970/1997; Giroux & McLaren, 1989);

2. teachers as public intellectuals (Giroux, 1988b);
3. curriculum based on experiences and voices of students (Shor, 1992; hooks, 1994);
4. emphasis on dialogue and consensus (Freire, 1970/1997; Ellsworth, 1988/1992; Lather, 1992);
5. pedagogy as praxis (Freire, 1970/1997; Lather, 1998; McLaren & Jaramillo, 2007); and
6. multiplicity and diversity (Luke & Gore, 1992; McLaren, 1997; Leonardo, 2002, 2005).

In addition, due to its interdisciplinary nature, critical pedagogy also encompasses diverse areas and topics outside these six core themes. However, largely influenced by the historical contexts of the time (i.e., critiques of the neo-Marxist theories and the influence of postmodernism), the two main agendas that have dominated critical pedagogy since its inception are: (1) knowledge/power and (2) pedagogy.

Knowledge and Power

The first and perhaps the most significant agenda of critical pedagogy is the relationship between knowledge and power. By asserting that knowledge is intrinsically interwoven with power, critical pedagogy adamantly and steadfastly dismisses the mainstream assumption of knowledge as objective and neutral. Based on this premise of the knowledge/power relationship, ideology critique and discourse analysis are employed as powerful conceptual tools in illuminating the interconnectedness of knowledge and power. Major power dynamics in society (i.e., class, race, and gender) are highlighted in this endeavor. From this process, critical pedagogy aims to construct alternatives to, or counter, hegemonic forms of knowledge, and therefore to change power.

On this, critical pedagogy is not only influenced by, but has also closely retained the core ideas of the neo-Marxist theories of education. In the late 1970s and the 1980s, a significant number of critical education studies emerged. These studies brought a new approach to school knowledge and curriculum, and challenged the mainstream educational paradigm. While the mainstream educational paradigm assumed knowledge to be objective, neutral, and given, and focused its curriculum studies largely on how best to organize and deliver predefined knowledge and skills to students, new critical theories raised a whole new set of questions, focusing on the ideological functions of school knowledge. Michael Apple (1979), while capturing the questions of the new curriculum theories, aptly and succinctly asks: but "*whose* knowledge?" and "for *whose* benefit and at *whose* expense?"

Critical education theories have subsequently developed new critical concepts. The "hidden curriculum" has been explored as a powerful apparatus for indoctrinating students through the routines of unspoken norms in daily school life and practices (Jackson, 1968; Apple, 1979; Giroux, 1988b). Additionally, the concepts of "habitus" and "cultural capital" have been articulated as mechanisms through which class hierarchy is (re)produced within the school knowledge system (Bourdieu & Passeron, 1977). Several empirical and theoretical studies have explored how hegemonic ideologies are embedded in and through school (Young, 1971; Apple, 1979). This new perspective on school curriculum ultimately fueled the "cultural war" between the Right and the Left regarding *which* knowledge and *whose* knowledge should constitute the official curriculum (Shor, 1992; Zavarzadeh & Morton, 1994). Controversies over

E.D. Hirsch's "cultural literacy" (1988) and the "standards of history" (Nash et al., 1997) are just two prominent examples of this cultural war over curriculum and school knowledge.

As such, the focus of critical pedagogy on the knowledge/power relationship is very much a continuation of, but also an elaboration on, earlier critical education theories. Then, is there anything new that critical pedagogy has added to what earlier critical education theories have already showed us about the relationship between knowledge and power? How is critical pedagogy's treatment of knowledge different from earlier critical education theories?

There are at least two differences. The first difference is multiplicity. Critical pedagogy has given better attention to gender, race, and other differences. Although neo-Marxist theories have usually included race and gender, along with class, in their paradigm, class has largely remained at the center. Studies on hidden curriculum, cultural capital, and the new sociology of curriculum (by Michael Young), have all placed class at the core of their theoretical frameworks. Critical pedagogy, however, has inserted multiplicity and diversity more forcefully into the study of knowledge and power. It has created spaces for multiple knowledges and multiple voices, especially for subjugated knowledges. From this, we have seen the birth of a number of studies, including Latino/a and red pedagogy, urban school, sexuality, and disability studies, and studies of other marginalities.

That said, it has to be noted that there have been some debates over the multiplicity of critical pedagogy. One has been the criticism of continuing class dominance within critical pedagogy. Feminists and anti-race theorists have lamented the relative neglect and marginalization of gender and race in critical pedagogy theories (Luke & Gore, 1992; Leonardo, 2005). Even so, I think it is fair to say that critical pedagogy is, or at least has the potential to be, more attentive to multiple marginalities than earlier critical education theories. Another issue with multiplicity has been the concern that the emphasis on multiplicity can create the problem of fragmentation and trivialization. For instance, Peter McLaren (1999) has argued that critical pedagogy has become a "whining contest." It is, according to him, as if everyone is trying to show that his/her marginality is the most important, or at least not any less important than any other marginalities. We all have some marginalities, and since we cannot assert that any one marginality is more significant than any other, we are all in the same boat. Of course, multiplicity does not need to be understood as "we are all the same," but if it does, then it will end up trivializing the very idea of marginality and oppression. And it must be said, there is, indeed, this tendency in critical pedagogy.

The other contribution of critical pedagogy to the studies of knowledge/power has been the concept of discourse and a more complex understanding of power. In examining the knowledge/power relationship, the key word for neo-Marxist education theories is "ideology/hegemony." The title of Apple's book, *Ideology and Curriculum* (1979), says it all. Critical pedagogy has replaced ideology with discourse. If a critical pedagogue would rewrite Apple's book, the title would be *Discourse and Curriculum.* The main reason for replacing ideology with discourse is, as Foucault (1980) points out, because ideology somehow still carries false consciousness and the concept of repressive power. By incorporating the concept of discourse, critical pedagogy has adopted a different understanding of power. Neo-Marxist education theories have been grounded on the concept of power as oppressive and negative power. Critical pedagogy, however, has included not only "negative" but also "positive" power.

This concept of power in critical pedagogy is an adaptation from poststructuralism. In poststructural and postmodernist concepts of power, power not only represses, prohibits, and reduces ("negative" power that says "no"), but power also "induces pleasure, forms knowledge, [and] produces discourse" (ibid.: 119). In this model, power constructs and creates meanings, feelings, identities, and desires ("positive" power that also says "yes"). This Foucauldian concept of power—which is power "beyond good and evil," a concept borrowed and adapted by Foucault from Nietzsche—obviously expands the operations and mechanisms of power into much wider fields beyond the institutions (thus, "power is everywhere," Foucault has declared). From this shift—from the "oppressive/repressive" power paradigm to the "productive" power paradigm—critical pedagogy has been able to go beyond the institutional levels of understanding of power, and to venture into areas that have not been previously studied, such as to feelings, desires, subjectivities, and identities. Power is understood to be much more pervasive in critical pedagogy than in neo-Marxist concepts/theories. To summarize, in its study of the relationship between knowledge and power, critical pedagogy is different from neo-Marxist education theories in two aspects: (1) multiplicity; and (2) differentiated conceptualizations of power.

The Democratization of Pedagogy

The other main agenda of critical pedagogy is the democratization of pedagogy, or more broadly, creating an emancipatory culture of schooling. Against the authoritarian and hierarchical power relations in classroom and school culture, critical pedagogy explores more democratic pedagogical arrangements and school cultures. The goal is "to critique and transform those classroom conditions tied to hegemonic processes that perpetuate the economic and cultural marginalization of subordinated groups" (Darder et al., 2003: 13). With this goal in mind, critical pedagogy studies have come forward to co-create curriculum with students, and to explore a more democratic or less authoritarian relationship between teachers and students. And this focus is what differentiates critical pedagogy from neo-Marxist education theories (thus the name, "pedagogy"). While earlier critical education studies have focused more on the macro-level analysis, critical pedagogy has paid more attention to the micro-level, namely teaching. As such, critical pedagogy has reconstructed the role of teachers. It has challenged the mainstream ideas of teachers, such as teachers as autonomous, neutral, and professional figures (thus, critiques on professionalism). Instead, critical pedagogy has redefined and extended the idea of roles of teachers and teaching. It has promoted teachers as cultural workers (Freire, 1970/1997; McLaren, 1989; Giroux, 1992) and teaching as a political act (Apple, 1979, 1982). In the same way, the role of students has also been redefined in critical pedagogy. Instead of passive recipients of knowledge (tabulae rasae), critical pedagogy has redefined students as cultural, political subjects (Freire, 1970/1997; McLaren, 1989; Giroux, 1992).

Freire's *Pedagogy of the Oppressed* (1970) has undoubtedly been the most influential work in this vein. Based on a resolute critique of "banking education," Freire proposes a "problem-posing" pedagogy for emancipatory education. Freire's influence has been both extensive and pronounced, and in many studies on schooling: *Empowering Education* by Ira Shor (1992); *Teaching to Transgress* by bell hooks (1994); *Rethinking Schools: An Agenda for Change* by Levine et al. (1995). In addition, we have witnessed a burgeoning of literature, focusing on emancipating and empowering pedagogy from feminist perspectives (Ellsworth, 1988/1992; Luke & Gore, 1992; Weiler & Mitchell, 1992; Macdonald & Sancher-Casal, 2002; Fine, 2003), and anti-racist perspectives (McLaren, 1997; Darder, Baltodano & Torres, 2003; Elenes, 2003; Allen, 2004; Grande, 2004; Leonardo, 2004, 2005).

This should already be clear, but one thing has to be emphasized: redefining and democratizing teaching is fundamentally a "political act" in critical pedagogy. The reason why critical pedagogy has redefined the roles of students and teachers is neither because respecting experiences and voices of students would make students more interested in learning, nor because it would motivate teachers to be more committed and caring. We all want interested and motivated students, as well as caring and committed teachers. But what critical pedagogy pursues is more than good teachers, good students, and good teaching. The political position—pedagogy as a political act, and schools and teachers as change agents—is what distinguishes critical pedagogy from liberal/progressive education (a point not always well understood).

Four Projects of Critical Pedagogy

As stated above, the major agendas of critical pedagogy are critical understanding of the relationship between knowledge and power, and democratization of school culture. How, then, are we to achieve these agendas? What projects has critical pedagogy presented in order to realize the emancipatory education it pursues? There are various ideas and propositions from individual critical pedagogues, and there exist nuanced differences among them. At the risk of over-generalization, I identify four projects that dominate critical pedagogy. For each project, I will attempt to capture its core ideas, discuss the major issues related to such ideas, and critically examine some of their problems and limitations. My analysis is based on critical pedagogy literatures, as well as my personal teaching experiences of critical pedagogy.

The Project of Experience

The first alternative project is what I call the "project of experience." When the hegemonic power of the system presents and enforces its own worldview as the natural and universal truth, how can we counteract such hegemonic claims, and from where can we explore alternatives? One source of exploration for critical pedagogy has been the lived "experiences" of learners. Building pedagogy and knowledge based on one's experience (students' experiences) is regarded as one way to counter the claims of hegemonic truth. The pedagogy of experience aims at "freeing students from oppressive cultural frames of knowing by providing them with new ways of claiming authority for their own experience[s]" (Zavarzadeh & Morton, 1994: 22). This is because, it is argued, the voices of those who are marginalized can/do provide "evidence for a world of alternative values and practices whose experience gives the lie to hegemonic constructions of social worlds" (Scott, 1992: 24). As such, according to Luke, the importance of experience in critical pedagogy has been paramount: "Agency and (raised) consciousness were reinstated on center stage, albeit this time with structural constraints acknowledged. *Lived experience* and intersubjective construction of meaning and identity formation were reauthenticated" (Luke, 1992: 26, emphasis added).

Claiming one's own experience is regarded not only as a process of ideology critique, but also as a way to find alternatives. As Darder, Baltodano, and Torres put it, "students come to understand themselves as subjects of history and to recognize that conditions of injustice . . . can also be transformed by human beings" (Darder et al., 2003: 12). The lived experiences and everyday modes of resistance are regarded as rendering possibilities against the "totalizing" reproductive nature of the system (e.g., Willis, 1977; Ong, 1987). The everyday small, yet significant, forms of resistance are conceived and celebrated as sources of possible challenges to, and eventual transformation of the system. In this way, *every voice* is regarded as emancipatory—or at least with the potential for emancipation—and *every resistance* is regarded as evidence for a rupture of power. In short, critical pedagogy focuses on the subject—their lived experiences and genuine voices—from which ideology critique, resistance, and alternatives are to be realized. There exist debates on what should constitute "experience," "genuine voices," and "resistance" (see Scott, 1992; Young, 2000). However, regardless of how one defines or conceptualizes "experience," "voice," or "resistance," it is generally agreed upon among critical pedagogues, at least those involved in the project of experience, that experience—especially students' experience—is where alternative emancipatory education should be pursued.

While many accept the importance of experience in critical pedagogy, there are some nuanced differences in understanding the project of experience. I can think of at least three different conceptualizations and approaches to experience. The first approach is experience for empowerment. On the most basic level, the project of experience is understood to empower students by validating their life experiences and their voices. If one takes the experience-for-empowerment approach, then critical pedagogy's project is very similar to, if not identical to, other pedagogies and learning theories, such as constructivism, experiential learning, or John Dewey's progressive education.

The second approach is experience for conscientization. If one takes the Freirean understanding of experience, then the project of experience goes deeper than empowerment in the ordinary sense of that term. It is not really about finding "who I am," or about feeling self-worth. Nor is it about learning from real experiences (experiential learning or "learning by doing"). Nor is it just about students' constructing knowledge and meaning (constructivism). For Freire's pedagogy, experience must mean more than just empowerment. Rather, the core element of Freire's *Pedagogy of the Oppressed* is about conscientization: the transformation of consciousness from an acceptance of oppression/reality to a belief that reality can be changed.

The third approach is experience for insurrection of subjugated knowledge. In this approach, constructing knowledge from students' experiences is understood as a way for an "insurrection of subjugated knowledge" (Foucault, 1980: 81). Foucault's concepts of the "subjugated knowledges" and the "regime of truth" are rather complicated concepts. To put it into simple terms, the revival of the subjugated knowledges means releasing the buried and disguised historical knowledges that are opposed to the effects of centralizing powers (ibid.: 84).

Thus, subjugated knowledges can challenge the hegemonic regime of truth. In this approach, the purpose of tapping into one's experience is to find and render the hidden historical knowledges, which are "capable of opposition and of struggle against the coercion of a theoretical, unitary, formal and scientific discourse" (ibid.: 85). A good example of this approach is Howard Zinn's _A People's History of the United States_ (1980).

The difference in the above three approaches is ultimately about the _purpose_ of experience: why experience matters; what we are trying to achieve through experience. And the three approaches each have a different explanation of why experiences are an important site for alternative projects. Certainly, it is possible to view these different approaches as neither incongruous nor contradictory, but rather as merely different in degree or level. If so, educators can start with empowering students by validating students' experience, and then based on that, go deeper to conscientization. As a final step, educators can aspire to release students' subjugated knowledges. This seems quite reasonable. However, a problem arises when one views the project of experience only as empowerment. There are some critical pedagogues—both in literature and in practice—who understand the project of experience as solely for empowerment of students. However, I believe (and hope) that both critical pedagogy and critical pedagogues strive for more than just "experience-for-empowerment." This, I think, is what ultimately separates critical pedagogy from "liberal" education.

Many critical educators may agree with the importance of experience/voices, and may accept the basic ideas of the project of experience. That said, there are, as in any discipline or project, issues and problems in mainstream critical pedagogy in how experiences and voices are understood and treated. I will point out two main problems. One problem is the issue of *essentialism*. In the rush to celebrate voices and differences, experience has become essentialized—experience now speaks for itself. Experiences and voices are treated as irreducible and the only legitimate basis for understanding. In a search for, and in honor of, genuine voices, the source of the voices becomes more important than the content of voices. In other words, "who speaks is what counts, not what is said" (Moore & Muller, 1999: 199). In critical pedagogy classrooms, who talks and what can be said become sensitive issues that can lead to and even create an atmosphere of fear and reluctance. No teacher or educator wants to be regarded as interrupting, let alone challenging, genuine voices of others—especially of minorities and women. Rather than making us more open and free, this essentialist interpretation of voices can actually create tension, and hamper honest communication and rigorous analysis. Furthermore, this essentialized voice discourse can be wrongfully perceived as anti-intellectualism. For instance, in my critical pedagogy courses, I have encountered some students who ask, "Why do we have to study dead white men's books? It has nothing to do with me." Students' suspicion of the dominance of white men in critical pedagogy theories, in tandem with their anger and resistance, are well justified. However, it is one thing to criticize the Euro-, male-, middle-class-, or heterosexual-centeredness in a given theory, but quite another to reject such theories on the sole basis that they are written by middle-class heterosexual white men (although I have to say there are close relations between these writings and writers).

Essentialism (and standpoint epistemology) has been fervently contested and challenged (see Nanda, 1997; Naples, 2003). It has been well established that experiences are social constructs. As Joan Scott points out: "[E]xperience is at once always already an interpretation and is in need of interpretation. What counts as experience is neither self-evident nor straightforward; it is always contested, always therefore political" (Scott, 1992: 37). Opening up critical pedagogy to include the voices and experiences of marginalized groups is no doubt crucial and necessary in critical pedagogy. However, uncritical glorification of experiences is also dangerous, even when the voices/experiences come from oppressed groups. Ilan Gur-Ze'ev warns:

> [T]his marginalized and repressed self-evident knowledge has no superiority over the self-evident knowledge of the oppressors. Relying on the knowledge of [the] weak, controlled, and marginalized groups, their memories and their conscious interests, is no less naïve and dangerous than relying on hegemonic knowledge.
>
> (Gur-Ze'ev, 1998: 480)

Another issue that is related to experience is *relativism*. Since experience speaks for itself, and since there are no absolute criteria for the truth, anyone's interpretation is as good as anyone else's: "anything goes." We see this relativist position, especially in "ludic" postmodernism (Ebert, 1996). That said, I do not mean to imply that the project of experience of critical pedagogy inevitably leads us to relativism. In fact, rejecting the "totalizing" truth claims of modernism does not necessarily mean subscribing to arbitrarism, relativism, or "debunking epistemology" (Moore & Muller 1999; Young, 2000). As Terry Eagleton points out, "[i]t is perfectly possible to agree with Nietzsche and Foucault that power is everywhere, while wanting for certain practical purposes to distinguish between more and less central instances of it" (Eagleton, 1991: 8). One can say, for example, criminals are more likely and are in a better position to see injustices of the legal system than judges or lawmakers, without resorting to an essentialist or totalizing position such as "all criminals always know better." Similarly, we are not falling into essentialism or totalizing modernist discourse when we say that "the level of food supplies in Mozambique is a weightier issue than the love life of Mickey Mouse" (ibid.). As Immanuel Wallerstein has aptly pointed out, "[t]o be against particularism disguised as universalism does not mean that all views are equally valid and that the search for a pluralistic universalism is futile" (Wallerstein, 2004a: 21).

The Project of Multiplicity and Inclusion

Closely related to the first, the second project of critical pedagogy is what I call the "project of multiplicity and inclusion." The emphasis on the multiplicity of subject/agency is a core foundation of critical pedagogy. It is a corrective response to the Marxist praxis, which tends to neglect or subordinate other forms of domination—race, gender, sexuality, and imperialism —to class (Butler, 1997; Leonardo, 2003a). Critique of racism, sexism, and other marginalities are a central focus of critical pedagogy. Therefore, in understanding and reclaiming students' experience, it is of utmost importance to pay close attention to the diverse social locations of students—again, that of class, race, gender, sexuality, religion, nationality, disability, and other marginalized statuses.

The main way to insert multiplicity into critical pedagogy is through inclusion. The aim of the inclusion project is to reform educational and other social institutions to make them more inclusive, and to do so based on desirable principles (i.e., equality, equal rights, anti-discrimination, democracy, emancipation, common goods, individual liberty, recognition, peace, or social justice). The guarantee of equal opportunity and equal power for the underprivileged, oppressed, marginalized, or subjugated is the ultimate goal of this project. Of course, the project of inclusion is not a new idea. As we know, multiculturalism and multicultural education is an effort for inclusion of the groups who have been excluded, discriminated, and marginalized. In a sense, the inclusion project of critical pedagogy can be understood as having a similar vein of reason as "rights-based" liberalism and multiculturalism. That is why, I believe, the word "inclusion" is not usually employed in critical pedagogy discourse. Rather, critical pedagogy uses terms such as "border-crossings," "between-borders," "border-less," "border-lands," or "border-ness" (Giroux, 1992; Giroux & McLaren, 1994; Darder et al., 2003). These new terminologies seem to be an attempt to differentiate and distance critical pedagogy from "rights-based" liberal multiculturalism. We have seen calls among critical pedagogues to go beyond the mainstream approaches of inclusion to more critical multiculturalist approaches: "insurgent multiculturalism" (Giroux, 1995); "revolutionary multiculturalism" (McLaren & Farahmandpur, 2001); and "subaltern cosmopolitan multiculturalism" (Buras & Motter, 2006).

Critical educators agree with the need for multiple marginalities and the project of inclusion. Sensitivity to all/diverse dynamics of power is acceptable and desirable to many. However, there are some controversies within and concerns with the project of multiplicity and inclusion. One issue is whether the border-crossing and radical multiculturalism in critical pedagogy is actually different enough to go beyond "rights-based" multiculturalism. More often than not, multiplicity politics of critical pedagogy are directed against the privileges of those in positions of power, rather than against the actual system of power/domination. Scatamburlo-D'Annibale and McLaren are very critical about this tendency in critical pedagogy: "[M]uch of what is called the 'politics of difference' is little more than a demand for inclusion into the club of representation—a posture which reinscribes a neoliberal pluralist stance rooted in the ideology of free-market capitalism" (Scatamburlo-D'Annibale & McLaren, 2004: 186). Furthermore, the discourse of equal rights and justice, as Benton points out, can easily become an ideology, a form of mystification, because "[i]n societies governed by deep inequalities of political power, economic wealth, social standing and cultural accomplishments, the promise of equal rights is delusory with the consequences that for the majority, rights are merely abstract, formal entitlements with little or no de facto purchase on the realities of social life" (Benton, 1993: 144). In short, the rights-based project is both slippery and risky, as it can easily end up a formality without real and substantial changes.

Another issue is that multiplicity in critical pedagogy has become dominated by personalized praxis and identity-based politics (Bourne, 1999). In her critique of the treatment of race in the British Centre for Cultural Studies, Jenny Bourne points out: "The 'personal is the political' also helped to shift the centre of gravity of struggle from the community and society to the individual. 'What has to be done?' was replaced by 'who am I?'. . . Articulating one's identity changed from being a path to political action to being the political action itself" (ibid.: 136). In other words, the problem is not the fact that critical pedagogy has moved to multiplicity—race/gender/sexuality/green/postcoloniality. Rather, the problem is that the multiplicity in critical pedagogy is too individualistic and not structural, and too culturalistic and not materialistic. Therefore, some critical educators (particularly neo-Marxists) criticize the idea of multiple marginalities for distracting our attention away from capitalism (and class), which they regard as the main conflict and contradiction within society. Neo-Marxists' concern is over the idea of including all marginalities, and treating all marginalities the same. Refusal to prioritize any marginality over any other can lead to essentialism and relativism. And, in so doing, rather than improving the power and position of the marginalized, this non-priority position of multiplicity can make our anti-system struggles fragmented and dispersed. As we know, this has been a point of tension among Marxists, feminists, and anti-racists.

However, as pointed out by some feminists and anti-racists, multiplicity and identity politics do not have to be either "merely cultural" (Butler, 1997) or to be reduced to "an individual's experience" (Leonardo, 2003a: 220). Indeed, some feminists and anti-racists argue that there is no reason to assume that critique of racism, sexism, or imperialism/postcolonialism cannot be a critique of the social structure. According to them, materialist analysis of other forms of power and oppression is not only possible, but also crucial in our critical understanding of vital connections among race, class, gender, and imperialism (e.g., Ahmad, 1995; Bourne, 1999; Connell, 1995). It is in this vein that, I think, the recent call to "go back to class" can be problematic, if it is understood as a call to prioritize class at the expense of race, gender, sexuality, disability, or global imperialism. Rather, I would argue that the call should be to transform the culturalized and personalized identitarian politics into "materialist identity politics" (Leonardo, 2003a: 220).

The Project of Anti-Hierarchy Democracy

Along with the projects of (1) experience and (2) multiplicity and inclusion, another way that critical pedagogy has been pursuing a "language of possibility" is what I call the "project of anti-hierarchy democracy." As mentioned above, one main agenda of critical pedagogy is to cultivate a democratic school culture. In order to create a genuinely democratic school culture, the first thing to do is to transform the authoritarian and hierarchical structures in schools. For this, critical pedagogy presents a nonhierarchical form of authority and participatory democracy. For instance, Patti Lather defines (and promotes) participatory, dialogic, and anti-hierarchical authority as the alternative form of authority in the "postmodernism of resistance" (Lather, 1991: 160). The focus of this project has been to find a democratic (hopefully power-free or less power-ridden) process of engagement. Thus, we have seen a proliferation of studies in feminist pedagogies on "politics of process": consensus, dialogue, pluralism, or celebration of differences (i.e., Luke & Gore, 1992; Ropers-Huilman, 1998; Mahler & Tetreault, 2002; Macdonald & Sancher-Casal, 2002).

As such, critical pedagogy focuses on power relations and authority structures in schools. These include relationships between school administrators and teachers, between teachers and parents, and teachers and students. Especially, critical pedagogy re-conceptualizes the relationship between teachers and students. It changes teachers from givers/authority figures to "co-learners" with students. Consequently, the emphasis has been on anti-authority and anti-hierarchy. This nonhierarchical, participatory form of authority is prevalent in critical pedagogy literature and praxis. There is a strong tendency to negate any structure or any possible hint of authority in critical pedagogy classrooms, as a way to achieve democracy and freedom, and to eliminate inequality and domination. Often, dialogue and consensus are regarded as the best, sometimes the only, legitimate and desirable form of decision-making. Among others, feminist critical pedagogues have been the pioneers in articulating the non-authoritarian structures of pedagogy.

This anti-hierarchy and anti-authority position of critical pedagogy is heavily influenced by poststructuralism and postmodernism, and more specifically by the Nietzschean and Foucauldian conceptions of power. Foucault, who adopted the concept of power from Nietzsche, presents a somewhat different conceptualization of power. Instead of seeing power as "possession," Foucault has maintained that it is more useful to see power as technology or mechanism. According to Foucault, what really matters is neither who has power (e.g., capitalists or the ruling class), nor where power is located (e.g., the state or Wall Street). Instead, the real focus should be on how power operates, and what mechanisms power employs (Foucault, 1980). The political implications of Foucault's theory of power are enormous. One implication is that power in modern Western society no longer operates exclusively through the state and the state apparatus. Therefore, replacing the repressive power of the state would not bring fundamental changes in the structure of power.

As such, this Foucauldian position leads us to the politics of anti-systematic change. We should no longer be so naive as to believe in the possibility of systemic changes via revolutions, according to this position. Instead of pursuing systemic changes, the only viable option left is local, grassroots democracy movements. Now, according to this Foucauldian position, the target of the struggle should not be the state, institutions, nor formal hierarchies of power, since changes in these institutions would not bring true transformation of society. So, the target of our struggle should be everyday lives and experiences, or at the molecular levels where power circulates and formulates subjects (thus, the famous phrase of Foucault, "power is everywhere"). Thus, with this abandonment of systematic changes (including the state), individual and local struggles have become the main site of social change.

That said, it should be noted that there have also been fervent debates among critical pedagogues on this question of power, hierarchy, and authority. To begin with, it needs to be pointed out that this is only one interpretation of Foucault. It is perfectly possible to accept Foucault's concept of power, and not reach this anti-system or relativist position (see Eagleton, 1991). Furthermore, there has also been skepticism surrounding the very idea of "hierarchy-free" and "power-free" critical pedagogy. As reviewed in Chapter 2, Ellsworth's article, "Why doesn't this feel empowering?" (1988/1992), has sparked debates on the question of whether and how critical pedagogy could be both power-free and genuinely empowering. Some critical pedagogy theorists—particularly feminists—have presented a post-structural critical pedagogy, arguing that it better presents an alternative to the "moralizing and totalizing" modernist critical pedagogy (Lather, 1992, 1998; Luke & Gore, 1992). Accordingly, to these critical pedagogy theorists, "power-free" or "less power-laden" critical pedagogy is both possible and attainable.

On the other hand, there are other postmodernists who are less sanguine about a critical pedagogy being free from power and hierarchy (Sidorkin, 1997; Biesta, 1998; Gur-Ze'ev, 1998). According to them, idealization of total freedom and the elimination of domination are utopian and naive. Alexander

Sidorkin argues that "no amount of care and justice" would change or eliminate the dominating nature of education (Sidorkin, 1997: 235). Similarly, Gur-Ze'ev, also skeptical about the idea of "power-free" pedagogy, writes:

> [T]he consensus reached by the reflective subject taking part in the dialogue offered by critical pedagogy is naive, especially in light of its declared anti-intellectualism on the one hand and its pronounced glorification of the "feelings", "experience", and "self-evident knowledge of the group on the other."
>
> (Gur-Ze'ev, 1998: 480)

Thus, instead of "empowering educaton," they have proposed a pedagogy of negation: counter-education as a non-repressive form of hope (Gur-Ze'ev, 1998), an emancipatory ignorance (Biesta, 1998), or pedagogy of carnival and of "third places" (Sidorkin, 1997). While the postmodern pedagogy of negation (mainly from Europe) may be unsettling to some critical educators, I think it is a useful antidote against romantic utopianism and easy optimism quite prevalent within the American critical pedagogy circles.

The Project of Individual Enlightenment

Another dominant project in critical pedagogy is what I call the "project of individual enlightenment." Fundamentally, what critical pedagogy targets is remaking individuals or subjectivities. The dominant versions of critical pedagogy treat the individual as the unit to be conscientized and propose allocating greater agency to individuals. Thus, critical pedagogues' job is to make students, as well as themselves, more aware of classism, sexism, racism, homophobia, and other forms of oppression and domination. I believe this is a widely accepted idea not only in critical pedagogy, but also in critical education in general. I often hear critical educators saying, "We have to educate ourselves and our students," with the belief that enlightened students and teachers can both make an impact on and change society. Henry Giroux aptly captures this idea: "[E]ducators play a crucial role in shaping the identities, values, and beliefs of students who impact directly upon society" (Giroux, 1997: 150). In short, critical pedagogy is based on the premise that emancipation can be realized when people have an adequate understanding of their own oppressive situations. The idea of changing students is simple enough, and many educators certainly share in that belief. Teachers often say that they want to make a difference to and in their students' lives. And I believe that the desire "to make a difference" is one of the main reasons why people choose to become teachers. In that sense, the project of individual enlightenment of critical pedagogy is pretty much the same as the "making a difference" belief among educators. Although this "making a difference" idea and the individual enlightenment premise of critical pedagogy may seem commonsensical to many, I think there are issues that need to be raised and carefully scrutinized, especially in critical pedagogy and among critical pedagogues.

One problem with the project of individual enlightenment is the "false consciousness thesis," which is, I think, rather prevalent in critical pedagogy. In my own teaching experiences of critical pedagogy, as well as in some of the mainstream critical pedagogy literature, I often see critical pedagogues fall prey to the "false consciousness thesis." To put it simply, this thesis posits that individuals are more or less caught up in their illusions, and if they were exposed to the "real truth," they would/could become enlightened. This simple and linear logic of the transition from illusion to enlightenment via conscientization seems to make critical pedagogues' job much easier. However, I do not think that this "false-consciousness thesis" provides an adequate insight into why people comply with the legitimization of an oppressive system. It may be helpful to remind ourselves of Gramsci's concept of hegemony. According to Gramsci, people conform to the system not because they fail to see their "real" interests (false consciousness), but because the ruling class is able to gain consent from dominated groups by hegemony and by making concessions (i.e., higher wages and shorter working hours). This does not mean that ideology does not involve some false consciousness, such as falsity, distortion, and mystification. Yet, as Terry Eagleton points out, "successful ideologies must be more than imposed illusions, and for all their inconsistencies must communicate to their subjects a version of social reality which is *real and recognizable* enough not to be simply rejected out of hand" (Eagleton, 1991: 15, emphasis added).

Even though many educators believe that schools should and could be "the great equalizer," they know, deep down, that this is not the reality. In other words, educators are not necessarily victims of false consciousness. Yet, it is rather amazing (and frustrating at the same time) to see how seamlessly they are able to not only absorb, but also incorporate the discrepancy between their beliefs and the reality into their mostly liberal perspectives. I believe that Peter Sloterdijk's theory on cynicism provides a better explanation for these educators' positions. Sloterdijk (1997) characterizes cynicism—the prevalent consciousness of western societies—to be an "enlightened false consciousness." According to Sloterdijk, people live with false values, but they are ironically aware of their falsity. To this prevalent cynicism, he argues, the ideology critique is rather powerless because "this consciousness no longer feels affected by any critique of ideology: its falsity is already reflectively buffered" (ibid.: 5). The sensibility of Americans, especially the white middle class, is too optimistic to be as cynical as Sloterdijk portrays. Yet, I think there is some truth to his characterization of the cynical consciousness of our time. If so, it may be that the consciousness of the conscientizer is more naive than that of the to-be-conscientized.

Another issue with the project of individual enlightenment is whether individual enlightenment would/could, in fact, bring social change. The project of individual enlightenment is based on a simple idea/assumption that enlightened individuals can impact society, and eventually bring social change. However, this simple assumption is only an assumption. While many agree that individual conscientization is doubtlessly important, there is no direct or necessary link between individual enlightenment and structural changes. Borrowing R.W. Connell's phrase, "[S]o much awareness is not the crumbling of the material and institutional structures" (Connell, 1995: 226). Awareness does not automatically bring the collapse of the system, and resistance does not necessarily bring new social arrangements. Critical teachers may "implement anti-racist teaching practices, but this does not, by itself, change the racist character of our educational system" (Shilling, 1992: 79).

Some point out that cultural and identity politics have contributed greatly to moving critical pedagogy in the direction of individualized projects. Certainly, they have. Yet, I believe that there is a more fundamental reason why individualized projects have come under the umbrella of critical pedagogy, which has often been overlooked. This emphasis on an

individualized project is very closely linked to the Western focus
on the ego and the concept of individualism, especially of the
white middle class. I believe that rugged individualism, one of
the strongest undercurrent hegemonies of American society,
is the reason why mainstream critical pedagogy has come so close
to liberalism, to the extent that it is sometimes hard to
distinguish between the two.

Concluding Remarks

Often, cultural theories and cultural politics are posited as
opposite to the studies of the economy or materialist theories.
The debates usually take an either/or approach: culture or
economy, superstructure or base, discourse or materiality. As
such, materialists often criticize cultural studies and cultural
politics for neglecting the material structures of society, de-
emphasizing the power and function of capital, and diminishing
the centrality of class. Culturalists, in return, often criticize
materialist theories for trivializing cultural and subjective
dimensions of society and for devaluing cultural studies and
cultural politics.

   We see the same debate in regards to critical pedagogy. On the
one hand, critical pedagogy has been criticized by poststructural feminists for basing its principles on liberal and Enlightenment modernism. For instance, Ellsworth claims that critical
pedagogy offers "only the most abstract, decontextualized
criteria for choosing one position over others, criteria such as
reconstructive action or radical democracy and social justice"
(Ellsworth, 1988/1992: 93). Similarly, Luke claims that the
basic concepts of critical pedagogy, such as "emancipatory self-
and social empowerment, and of emancipatory rationality and

citizenship education[,] have been articulated in epistemic relation to liberal conceptions of equality and participatory democracy" (Luke, 1992: 29). And poststructural feminists' target of criticism has been neo-Marxist theories, which, as far as they see, are the theoretical bases of critical pedagogy. On the other hand, critical pedagogy has been criticized by neo-Marxists for couching itself too much in postmodernism and culturalism. According to neo-Marxists, cultural politics and postmodernism are problematic because they neither address nor provide a solution to major "structural" issues of inequality that dominate the educational system and society. Thus, McLaren argues that postmodern culturalism is the main reason why critical pedagogy can no longer provide a viable alternative for social change.

My intention in this chapter has been to go beyond these theory-level debates. Rather, what I have attempted to do is to figure out what alternatives critical pedagogy has proposed as its "language of possibility." And I have identified four main alternative projects in critical pedagogy. The project of experience is about where we can find critiques on hegemony and pursue counter-hegemonic knowledges, and it is within the students' experiences that critical pedagogy believes that we can find the "language of possibility." The project of multiplicity and inclusion is about how we can address the multiple marginalities, which is one of the essential concepts of critical pedagogy. The project of anti-hierarchy democracy is about how we can realize democratic school cultures, and the position of critical pedagogy is anti-hierarchical and participatory democracy. Finally, the project of individual enlightenment is about how we can promote social change, and critical pedagogy's position is that schools can be change agents via transformation of their students.

As critical pedagogy emerged both within and alongside the political and theoretical contexts that aimed to counteract the structural and economic determinism of earlier critical educational theories, it is only logical that critical pedagogy has turned to *agency* (against structural determinism), and to *culture* (against economic determinism). These redirections have led critical pedagogy to micro-level politics (individuals, classrooms, and teachings), where educators supposedly have direct impact. By this, I do not suggest that critical pedagogy theorists have only promoted micro-centered pedagogy and politics. In fact, they have also consistently argued for the link between pedagogy and the larger power dynamics of the society. However, as it stands today, much of the critical pedagogy literature and praxis still focuses on classroom pedagogy and agency.

As such, critical pedagogy is strong in the analysis of knowledge/power and teaching, but it is relatively weak in policy analysis and structural issues of education. The political economy, policy study, and political struggle against capital and the state are neither very visible nor very popular in critical pedagogy. It is, therefore, not surprising that critical pedagogy, in its current form, rarely addresses structural and systemic issues related to schools, such as finance, organizations, governance, the school board, bureaucracy, the teachers' union, politics of professionalism, national funding, educational policy, privatization, charter schools, and school choice. Furthermore, the individualized orientation in mainstream critical pedagogy is problematic, not only because it is naive, but also because it can lead to a moralized, rather than a politicized, project. By moralization, I mean an approach of identifying a social issue as a moral problem and prescribing a moral solution. The problem with the moralized approach is that it fails to address the issue in the broader social, political, economic, and cultural contexts, and thus prohibits us from searching for practical and structural solutions.

Cultural politics and identity politics, and its embodiment of grassroots democracy in critical pedagogy may seem both genuine and ideal. However, if grassroots, localized, and issue-oriented politics neglect or avoid major structural issues of inequality, oppression, and exploitation, then I think it is both dangerous and ultimately powerless. Furthermore, I do not see culturalized and self-oriented identity politics as counter-hegemonic politics, but rather as a reflection of the defeated consciousness of Western postmodern society, which believes neither in revolution nor in any other structural changes.

In addition, the "personal" and the "local" cannot be viable alternatives to growing imperial globalization (Amin, 1997). The politics of identity/differences is actually what flexible global capitalism endorses and promotes (Castells, 1996; Castells et al., 1999; Hardt & Negri, 2000). Perhaps critical pedagogues of the North are able to afford exploring and celebrating identities and differences. However, celebration of identity and differences may have little relevance to many people of the South whose daily lives are severely threatened by neoliberal, imperial capitalism. The fragmentation and marginalization within identity politics —which cater to the "center," while neglecting the realities of the "peripheries"—cannot account for everyone's experiences and differences, as identity politics claims to do. Rather, identity politics has been plagued by the same Euro-/First-World-centrism as the universalizing and totalizing claims of modernism, from which identity politics desperately sought to break away. This contradiction has corrupted the basic tenets of diversity and differences upon which identity politics were initially founded. In short, identity politics is a winner's politics based on privilege.

Students do not change just because they are told to change. Similarly, teachers do not change just because they encounter the "truth." Individuals change their moralities, values, and behaviors when social structures are conducive to and can support such changes. The real task of critical pedagogy is to create the social structures that allow individuals to change and to grow. Rather than focusing on reforming individuals per se, critical pedagogy should explore alternative visions of social structures and conditions, so that ordinary teachers and students can practice and experience a pedagogy of hope, love, equality, and social justice. If, however, a pedagogy of hope, care, love, and social justice is understood to be a project of (re)making or (re)forming teachers and students, it would necessarily limit, rather than expand, the exploration of possibilities for alternative politics. Furthermore, this individualized and moral orientation in mainstream critical pedagogy, I believe, is also dangerous, especially given today's rapid imperialistic globalization. Rather than going back to the body, the individual, and the subjectivities, which the Western thought has been so terribly plagued with, what critical pedagogy needs to do in its search for "possibilities" is to explore and produce real feasible alternatives, by linking the micro to the macro, the subject to the structure, the culture to the economy, and the local to the global.

5

EDUCATIONS OF RESISTANCE AGAINST GLOBALIZATION

Introduction

This chapter focuses on recent education literature on globalization as another important venue in exploring the "language of possibility." Of course, studies on globalization are not, by any means, a monopoly of critical pedagogy, and not all critical pedagogy studies deal with globalization. Globalization studies in education go beyond the boundary of critical pedagogy, especially if one defines critical pedagogy at the micro-level, as classrooms and teaching. If one defines critical pedagogy more broadly, then globalization would fit right into critical pedagogy. Whichever definition one takes, I believe critical pedagogy has a lot to learn from globalization studies, in its search for a "language of possibility." It is because, as critical education takes the challenges of neoliberal globalization, it is compelled to come up with alternative visions of education against the neoliberal globalization.

In the previous chapters, I have examined how critical pedagogy has framed its "language of possibility" during the 1980s and the 1990s. I have argued that critical pedagogy has heavily couched its alternatives in cultural politics and body discourse. This theoretical leaning of critical pedagogy has been influenced by the academic discourses during that time. If one attempts to identify the most dominant post-1970s topics, they would be "the body" and "the globalization" (Harvey, 2000). However, critical pedagogy has been almost exclusively influenced by the former. It has rarely incorporated globalization literature until very recently (Castells, et al., 1999; Apple, 2000; Burbules & Torres, 2000; Allman, 2001; Apple et al., 2005; Lissovoy, 2008; Spring, 2008b; Apple, 2010). Preoccupied with the politics and signification of the body, critical pedagogy has been pushed in a certain direction. Against structural determinism, critical pedagogy has been shifted to rediscover human agency, which has been all but denied or woefully ignored in structural determinism. As such, it has focused on the subject—lived experiences, voices, and resistance.

Recently, however, a new theme has emerged in academic discourse. This new theme is globalization. Since the 1990s, we have seen an outpour of studies on globalization. If the body has been the theme of the 1980s and the 1990s, globalization has become, or has been added to, the theme of academic discourse since the 1990s. The emergence of the globalization theme has done more than just adding a new topic to academic discourse. It has brought a significant shift of theoretical paradigm. During the 1980s and the 1990s when the body has been the dominant theme, discourse analyses and cultural studies have been the most popular fields of study. As such, poststructuralism and postmodernism have been the most dominant theoretical frameworks. Structural theories and political economy have been criticized as "totalizing modernism." Not long ago, materialist theories, particularly Marxism, were criticized as being vulgar. With globalization, however, we have seen the re-emergence of the materialist theories and political economy. By this, I do not mean to suggest a complete shift of theories or methodologies, from the culturalist to the materialist, or from postmodernism to Marxism. Cultural theories and body politics have not disappeared. Rather, what I am suggesting is that due to global expansion of neoliberal capitalism, the academic discourse now deals with material analysis and political economy, in addition to cultural studies and identity/body politics.

We see the same shift of this trend in education. In recent years, globalization has been receiving keen interest within education studies. There are several valuable studies that examine and synthesize diverse conceptualizations of globalization and different responses to globalization, such as Burbules and Torres (2000), Stromquist and Monkman (2000), Tikly (2001), Carnoy and Rhoten (2002), Chan-Tiberghien (2004), Apple et al. (2005), Fischman et al. (2005), Spring (2008b), and Apple (2010). We have seen growing critiques on global capitalism and neoliberal educational reforms. In this endeavor, special focus has been given to neoliberalism, marketization and privatization, global culture, standards, testing, and No Child Left Behind (NCLB).

Before we move on, perhaps it would be helpful to briefly recap a few key points that studies on globalization have taught us so far. Several studies have pointed out that globalization creates not only a convergent trend, but also a divergent trend. Global integration and global education reforms have turned education into some universal forms (such as more privatization, marketization, and standardization), but there have also been considerable divergent responses to globalization in different countries. Therefore, the globalization process and global educational reforms are not monolithic, but complex and diverse. For instance, Apple et al. (2005) point out that globalization is a complex process, involving contradictions, resistances, and countervailing forces. Therefore, according to them, globalization is better understood not as a uniform process, but as a process of complex connectivity (this is the core idea of the complex connectivity theory). Just as globalization is a complex process, reactions and resistance to globalization are also diverse. For example, Burbules and Torres (2000) show us that it is useful to distinguish anti-globalization from counter-globalization, to understand them as two different reactions to globalization.

Therefore, contrary to a common claim that we have become one via a global village, we need to notice that there are diverse and different interpretations of globalization, and one's response to globalization can vary and differ according to the interpretation. For instance, Joel Spring (2008b) identifies four interpretations of globalization:

1. world culturalist (neo-institutionalist), which sees globalization as a process of all cultures being integrated into a single global culture;
2. world systems theory, which regards globalization as a process to legitimize the powers and actions of rich nations by inculcating their values into periphery nations;

3. postcolonialist, which views globalization as an effort to impose particular economic and political agendas that benefit rich nations on the global society; and

4. culturalist, which considers globalization as a process of local actors borrowing from multiple models in the global flow of educational ideas.

As for alternatives to neoliberal globalization, critical education has branched off into different directions. Diverse ideas and theories have been presented, such as utopianism, humanism, existentialism, democracy, popular culture, and local diversity. Along with these ideas/theories, many pedagogies are presented as alternatives: public pedagogy, critical public pedagogy, revolutionary pedagogy, pedagogy of hope, pedagogy of possibility, pedagogy of humanity, pedagogy of liberation, utopian pedagogy, indigenous pedagogy, postcolonial pedagogy, place-based pedagogy, and critical pedagogy of place. My aim here is not to review all of these alternative pedagogies. Rather, what I want to do is to synthesize diverse ideas and pedagogies, with the aim to elucidate main directions and trends in such alternative pedagogies. In order to do that, my approach is to identify what these alternatives are arguing *against*: what do they see as the main problems of neoliberal globalization? How one defines a problem inevitably shapes what alternatives one comes up with. So, the first job is to clarify how critical education conceptualizes the key problems with neoliberal globalization. Then, from there, we can move to the next step, and identify what they are advocating *for*: where do they go to find a way out? The reason why I choose to start with "against" is because often we assume, rather than articulate, the main problems we are facing. I hope that by focusing on the "against," we can sort through seemingly diverse ideas, and can extract larger trends that underlie the diverse ideas. In this chapter, I focus on five major issues/problems that critical education is addressing: (1) TINA (There Is No Alternative), (2) instrumentalism and dehumanization, (3) single global culture (universalism), (4) global capitalism, and (5) Western colonization, and five corresponding alternative positions that have been presented as their solutions: utopianism, humanism, localism, globalism, and postcolonialism.

TINA (There Is No Alternative): Utopians

The fall of the Berlin Wall (1987) and the collapse of the Soviet Union (1989) marked the end of an era, the cold war era. This signified, some have claimed, the final triumph of capitalism, ending the ideological war between capitalism and socialism (thus, called "the end of ideology"). Some have gone even farther. The collapse of the Soviet Union and Eastern Europe, they argue, is proof that capitalism is the ultimate and final form of socio-economic system. There is no other, or no better, system, and therefore there is no next stage for history to move onto. All we are left to do is to improve what we have. "This is it" is what they are saying. Therefore, they maintain that we have finally reached "the end of history." Margaret Thatcher, then British Prime Minister, captured this triumphant view by coining the famous (or infamous) phrase, "There Is No Alternative" (TINA). Many, even in the Left, agree that an era indeed ended around 1989–1991. For instance, Immanuel Wallerstein (2004a) recognizes that the modern era ended in 1989. Eric Hobsbawm (1994) also marks the year of 1991 as the end of the 20th century. However, what they do not agree with is the claim that this end of an era signaled the ultimate triumph of capitalism, and that there are no longer other alternatives to capitalism. Quite contrary, they both maintain that the end of the era is the end of capitalism, the process of the collapse of capitalism and liberalism. According to them, the current global financial crisis is the symptom of the transitional stage we are going through after capitalism and liberalism (Amin, 1997, 2004; Wallerstein, 2004a; Harvey, 2010).

However, despite the Left's dissent, the dominant trend has been the conservatives' claims and the rise of new conservatism since the later 1980s. With that, we have witnessed a sharp decline of Left politics in the 1980s and 1990s. Union membership has declined sharply, and progressive movements have weakened (Davis, 1999). The Left has become isolated, marginalized, and disillusioned. Thus, the utmost task for the new social movements has been to fight against and dispel this "TINA syndrome." Against the prevalent TINA, the first thing to do is to show that there are other alternatives, neoliberal capitalism is not inevitable, and other forms of society and world are indeed possible. That is why the World Social Forum's slogan is "Another World is Possible" (George, 2004; Mertes, 2004; Leite, 2005; Santos, 2006).

We see the same fight against the TINA mentality in critical education as well. For the last two to three decades, we have seen the market logic creeping into education. The education reform movements since the 1980s have couched their ideas in privatization, marketization, standardization, accountability, efficiency, and competition. The dominant responses to globalization were also largely about competition—how to compete and survive in the more globalized and competitive world, and how to best adjust to the information/knowledge economy. Amid these discourses of competition (standardized testing, data-driven, evidence-based), it is hard to even imagine an alternative education that is not about competition. It is within this overwhelming mood of the TINA syndrome that we see searches for other possibilities and hopes. Ideas such as the "pedagogy of possibility" and "pedagogy of hope" are manifestations of this very need. This is why the word "possibilities" is used and circulated more often these days, as in "Radical Possibilities" by Jean Anyon (2005), and "Another School is Possible" (Wrigley, 2006).

Among others, I think "utopian pedagogy" would be a good example to combat TINA syndrome in education. One route to combat the TINA despair is to go beyond and imagine outside the current logic of neoliberalism. This is what the "utopian pedagogy" is about (Peters & Freeman-Moir, 2006; Cote et al., 2007). In their edited book *Utopian Pedagogy*, Cote, Day, and Peuter explain the need for utopia and utopian pedagogy: "[U]topian theory and practice acquire a new relevance, as the hyperinclusive logic of neoliberalism compels us to take up positions that are intrinsically outside of and other than what is" (Cote et al., 2007: 4). And that which is "outside of and other than what is," is what they call utopian pedagogy. In short, the basic idea of utopia is to *transcend* what is conceivable within the current socio-economic order. In their edited book *Edutopias: New Utopian Thinking in Education*, Peters and Freeman-Moir succinctly capture the reason for the engagement of utopian idea/pedagogy in education theory: "the left must also find ways to articulate possibilities for the future" (Peters & Freeman-Moir, 2006: 12).

The idea of utopian pedagogy ("what is beyond what is") is very abstract and broad. Many ideas could be conceived of as utopian pedagogy. For instance, Cote, Day, and Peuter's book

(2007) includes a variety of pedagogy ideas as utopian pedagogy, from the project of educated hope (Giroux), revolutionary learning (Boren), exiled pedagogy (Zaslove), the diffused intellectuals (Costa), transformative social justice learning (Torres), and anarchist pedagogy (Antliff). Peters and Freeman-Moir's book (2006) also surveys a variety of perspectives and theories on utopia and utopian education. In a way, all alternative education and critical pedagogies are utopian pedagogy, in the sense that they all present alternatives against the mainstream, currently neoliberal education frameworks. As Zeus Leonardo (2006) has aptly pointed out, "ideology critique often projects an alternative reality, a utopia, and that utopian thinking is inherently a form of ideology critique." I think the broadness of utopian pedagogy has both strength and weakness. On the one hand, the broad and abstract definition opens up creative and unconventional thinking, stretching our imagination to go beyond the boundaries of what seems feasible. As it is intended, it compels us to imagine beyond the boundaries that have been imagined, and think beyond the boundaries that have been previously thought: thus into utopia. In that sense, the idea of utopian pedagogy resembles the "regime of truth" of Foucault (1980). On the other hand, a problem with utopian pedagogy is that what it advocates in more concrete terms is not at all clear. How to transplant "utopian" education ideas into concrete education policies and practices remains to be better articulated.

Instrumentalism and Dehumanization: Humanists

To some, the fundamental problem with globalization and global capitalism is intensification of instrumentalism and dehumanization. The instrumentalism of modernity and capitalism has

brought many technical advancements and material con-
veniences. However, these advancements have come at the price
of dehumanization. Fetishism, alienation, and dehumanization
are not new or unique problems of the neoliberal globalization
of the last 30 years or so. This is a fundamental and broad-scale
issue of modern, capitalist life. What is new with the current
neoliberal globalization is the intensification of dehumanization
with the geographical extension of capitalism. During the last
three decades, the commercialization logic of market capitalism
has found its way further and deeper into public fields. "The
public is bad and the private is good" has been the drumming
maxim to drive privatization of public services. In the U.S., where
public services are comparatively small, a few of the remaining public services have become the target of reform. This is
why we have seen reform movements in the last three decades,
particularly targeted at welfare, health care, and education.
Furthermore, the logic of capitalism has permeated more
and more into "private" life. Now we not only sell goods and
products, but personalities, feelings, and smiles.

As we know, commodification and privatization have seeped
into education. For the last 30 years or so, we have been satur-
ted with talk of accountability, standards, tests, privatization,
marketization, and commercialization. High-stakes testing has
become mandatory for accountability and efficiency. Students'
scores are used to evaluate (and eventually eliminate) failing schools. Merit pay has been introduced as an incentive to
differentiate teachers based on their performance, and to bring
competition among teachers. The tenure system for teachers
has been hotly debated and challenged, identified as a cause of
mediocre teaching quality. Voucher and school choices have
been revived to make schools compete for funding. Private

companies have come to rescue "failing schools," with the logic that schools would be better off if they are run like private companies. Now some schools in the U.S. are run by private companies, with the bottom line of making a profit ("schools-for-profit"). These educational reform initiatives in the U.S., particularly "NCLB," have been challenged and criticized for various reasons, from practical implementation problems to more fundamental and philosophical reasons. Many argued that the current educational policies in the U.S. result in negative consequences, such as "teaching to the tests," cultural biases in standardized tests, unfair evaluation for disadvantaged schools and teachers, and punishment-oriented incentives (such as decrease of school funding and school closing). However, to some people, the problem of the current education trend is more fundamental, which is the expansion and deepening of instrumentalism and dehumanization in the education field.

Of course, instrumentalism is not new only to the current neoliberal educational reform. As Michael Apple (1979) and many others have pointed out, instrumental rationale has dominated American schools from the beginning. However, what is new and alarming this time is the extensiveness and pervasiveness of instrumentalism and dehumanization. Although instrumental rationale has been the basis of American schools (and of the American society in general), the emphasis on instrumentalism and efficiency in recent times has been heavier and more one-sided than in the past, to the point that it is hard to imagine schooling and education as preoccupied with anything other than efficiency and instrumentalism. As Pinar aptly remarks, "it is difficult to remember that the school was once imagined as a laboratory for democracy, a bulwark against an unjust and oppressive world" (Pinar, 2010: xvi).

Critical education hazards many theories to address and over-come this deepening instrumentalism and dehumanization. The ideals and principles of humanism and existentialism are articu-lated, revived, and utilized to seek out education that is human and humane, beyond just an instrument and a commodity. Recent interest in ideas such as pedagogy of humanity (Sandlin et al., 2010) and pedagogy of care (Noddings, 2005) are mani-festations of, and attempts to preserve, humanity and being fully human. Others have revisited Marxism for humanization (Allman, 2001, 2007; McLaren & Jaramillo, 2007). For instance, Allman (2001) lists the "project of humanization" as one of the principles of and aims for critical education for revolutionary social transformation. While there are differences in how and from where they have pursued the revision of humanism, I call them "humanists," because they share the fundamental idea of problematizing the instrumentalism and dehumanization of the neoliberal education trend of our time. Of course, humanist education is not new. Education based on humanism has been long promoted. It is clearly presented as the historical vocation of humanization by the oppressed in Paulo Freire's *Pedagogy of the Oppressed* (1970/1997). Maxine Greene's focus on exis-tentialism (Greene, 1967), freedom (Greene, 1988), and arts (Greene, 1995) are essentially attempts to fight against the dehumanizing spirit of modernity. So what we are witnessing is the revival of this tradition of humanist thought in education as a resistance against the neoliberal educational movements. As such, the ideals of freedom, equality, justice, peace, and democ-racy are being revived, salvaged, and reinvented.

This is a very interesting phenomenon, since it is this Enlightenment modernism/humanism that poststructuralism and postmodernism has been problematizing and criticizing since the 1970s. I am not suggesting the ideas of democracy, social justice, and freedom have been abandoned, or that they have disappeared from critical education since the 1970s. These ideas have always been present, and have been echoed in many concepts in critical education. But, not long ago, modernism and humanism were almost taboo among critical theorists. Any theories based on modernism were criticized as "grand narratives," or "meta-narratives." And the grand narratives (both Enlightenment narratives and Marxist narratives) were criticized and rejected for totalism/universalism, as grand narratives do "violence to the heterogeneity" of knowledge/truth (Lyotard, 1984: xxv). Now that humanism is being revived and recirculated in critical education, I cannot help but think of Lyotard's merciless critique of high modernism, and Foucault's caution against moral and ideological ideas such as social justice. After several decades of critique and skepticism, it would be interesting to see how these ideals are to be reconstructed. Furthermore, humanism and humanist pedagogy can become problematic and slippery, in that these ideas and words have been hijacked by the Right. As we know, the abstracts of democracy, freedom, and peace have been used to justify wars and invasions in recent years. With such corruption of these ideals, it is not easy to view these words without reservation and suspicion. In the end, the question is how (or whether) these modernist/humanist ideas can be reconstructed without the Eurocentrism that has been so deeply embedded within them.

Global Culture as Universalism: Localists

The approach to globalization is diverse and complex. At one end of the spectrum, globalization is viewed as a positive step toward global economic development and global integration. At the other end, globalization is viewed as a negative trend toward global domination and exploitation. Critical education generally views globalization with critical or at least suspicious eyes. Among many critiques on neoliberal globalization, some consider the biggest problem with globalization to be globalism/universalism. According to this position, globalization not only destroys diversity by homogenizing global culture, but also legitimizes the power and actions of rich nations, by inculcating its values into periphery nations (Spring, 2008b). In other words, this position sees not only the current neoliberal form of globalization as problematic, but globalization itself as a dangerous phenomenon and thus to be resisted. In short, this is an *anti*-globalization position.

Therefore, the anti-globalizationists do not see replacing the neoliberal global education system with another global one as the solution. Instead, they see a localist approach as the alternative. They argue for replacement of the current neoliberal and developmentalist educational model, by recognizing multiple knowledges, alternative cultural frameworks for schooling, and the importance of studying the interaction between the local and the global (ibid.). For instance, Gruenewald and Smith (2007) call for "place-based education" as an alternative to globalization. What is needed, according to them, is to envision and change the process of education in tune with and connected to the sustainability of community life. Place-based education is "a community-based effort to reconnect the process of education, enculturation, and human development to the well-being of community life" (ibid.: xvi). Similarly, Peter Trifonas (2003) calls for including recognition of the value of difference, in what he terms "pedagogy of differences." According to Trifonas, the recognition of difference should be the basis "in efforts to articulate educational reform for achieving democracy and social justice" (ibid.: 2). What the localists represent is a recent focus in the new social movements on localism, diversity, differences, and an increasing focus on quality of life, sustainability, and ecology. In fact, some localists include the importance of sustainability and ecology in their alternative educational paradigm. For instance, Li (2003) advocates a "bioregion-based education," which stresses preserving local ecological systems, and establishing a bond between the members of a local community and their place. Similarly, ecology and sustainability are presented as the key idea of "eco-pedagogy" by Richard Kahn (2010). Ecology and sustainability are key issues that I believe we will see increasingly in the coming years.

While all localists acknowledge the importance of specificities and diversities of local, there seems to be some nuanced differences among localists. One camp, which I call local-localists, emphasizes the preservation of local diversities and the enhancement of community life. They are suspicious of a global logic of universalism and accumulation. To this camp, the local and the global is, in essence, oppositional or exclusionary (local against global). By focusing on places and local community, what this camp attempts to do is to foster a different lifestyle and vision of society. For instance, they emphasize sustainability and happiness. For this position, diversity is inherently better, and thus to be protected and promoted.

There are other localists, whom I call "glocalists," who emphasize the close link between local and global. It is not that they do not emphasize the specificities and diversities of the local. They do. But they do not necessarily see the local and the global as an opposing dichotomy. Since postmodern society is both global and local, many emphasize the importance of a local approach/project, without losing sight of the global dimension. Their point is how closely the two are becoming linked. That is why some use the term "glocal" to highlight the overlapping or inseparable aspect of global and local. This is one of the main arguments of *Empire*, a much-debated book by Hardt and Negri (2000). The significance and meaning of local for this position is that any social change and movement is, and has to be, always situated in a specific locale with global connectedness and influences.

For instance, Michael Apple suggests that we need to "develop a political project that is both local yet generalizable without making Eurocentric, masculinist claims to essential and universal truths about human subjects" (Apple, 2000: 13). The same sentiment is echoed by others. In attempting to revive radical political economy through Foucault, Olssen and Peters argue that "for Foucault, in a world that is both global and local the drive for change must take the form of resistance and struggle in specific sites, utilizing complex technologies and intellectual tools" (Olssen & Peters, 2007: 169). To some, the ultimate idea is to come up with some global or general elements through local specificities. To them, the local is seen as a way/path to the global and the general. To put it simply, some see the local as the destiny (local-localists), while for others the locals are more like a route to the destiny ("glocalists").

As reviewed in previous chapters, localism has been popular among new social movements. Yet, there have been some concerns and contentions on localism and local politics. A thorny issue for the localist approach is the potential negative consequences of differences. For instance, Peter Trifonas cautions the dangers in promoting differences as a way to achieve alternative education for social justice. While there is certainly a need to recognize differences, Trifonas argues that there is also "the need to try to bridge the negative values of difference that create competing theoretical and pedagogical discourses conducive neither to the principle or educational equity nor to education for social justice" (Trifonas, 2003: 3). Celebration of difference and localist education can create inequalities and imbalances. Without some mechanisms of coordination, pedagogy of differences can actually increase inequalities, and thus result in social injustice. As I understand it, the idea of "glocal" is an attempt to resolve this conflict between the local and the global, and between the particular and the universal, although the concept of "glocal" is rather elusive.

Global Capitalism: Globalists

This position, like others above, is also critical of neoliberal globalization, but it is not critical of globalization/globalism per se. This position acknowledges that global circulation of knowledge, technology, and culture can help to overcome parochialism, and bring forth a cosmopolitan consciousness and global network. A good example of this possibility of a global network is the rise of transnational social movements, such as the Green movement and ecological awareness. In addition, for economic development, globalization is seen as a maturing (and final) stage of capitalist development, which is a necessary and desirable phenomenon. This is based on the logic that capitalism has to be fully developed into a global system, in order to advance to the next stage, a kind of after/beyond capitalism (Amin, 1997, 2004). Thus, the problem, according to this position, is not the fact that we are becoming globalized.

Rather, the problem is the kind of globalization that is occurring now (i.e., the neoliberal globalization). This position is found in education. Some acknowledge that there are advantages and potential contributions with global education movements. To them, the real problem is not the globalizing trend in education, but the kind of globalizing education reform that is happening now (i.e., the human capital education reform movement). Thus, this position promotes the replacement of the neoliberal education paradigm with other (more progressive) global forms of schooling designed to empower the masses. To put it differently, this position is of *counter*-globalization, not of *anti*-globalization.

Then, what kind of global education should we pursue? What principles ought to guide in constructing a better global education system? There are several differing ideas among globalists, but they can be categorized into two camps, based on the principles of global education paradigm. The first camp, which I call the modernists, presents a global education paradigm based on modernist universal principles, such as democracy, human rights, or social contract. Some try to reconstruct democracy into a global and universal principal, by separating out nationalism and the nation-state from the modern construct of democracy (e.g., Reid, 2005). Similarly, Peters and Roberts (2000) propose to construct a "global social contract" as an alternative form of global education. Essentially, Peters and Roberts' proposal is to extend the "social contract" theory, which is a theory on the formation of the modern state, to the global scale. Lechner and Boli (2005) focus on culture, arguing that what needs to be done is to build a "global culture" based on human rights and environmental activism.

The second camp is to build an alternative global education paradigm based on socialism. Recently, socialism and Marxism are gaining traction in critical education, as well as in academia in general (perhaps a renaissance). Paula Allman advocates "a form of critical education—one that I often refer to as revolutionary critical education—that is capable of preparing people to take part in the creation of what I call authentic socialism: a society engaged in revolutionary social transformation and the development of the type of communist social formation advocated by Karl Marx" (Allman, 2001: 162). Peter McLaren is unequivocal in promoting "global socialism," a new transnationalism that extends beyond nation-state (McLaren & Farahmandpur, 2005; McLaren & Jaramillo, 2007). McLaren and Farahmandpur call for a radicalization of critical pedagogy, to become what they call "contraband pedagogy." Critical pedagogy, they insist, "must build a new vision of society freed from capital's law of value," and must endorse efforts "to build new international anti-capitalist struggles along the road to socialism" (McLaren & Farahmandpur, 2005: 150).

These globalists differ over what global models of schooling should be built, and some of these differences are vast. For instance, there may not be much common ground between global socialism and global democracy. However, what is common among them is the need to come up with an alternative global system/model of schooling. This globalist position may draw criticism and skepticism in that any global educational system gets into the problem of meta-narratives (universalism) (i.e., imposing one's truth and values on others). On top of that, Eurocentrism and Western colonization can be a thorny issue, since it is very hard to separate Eurocentrism out from universalism as we have known it. Of course, not all universalism is Eurocentric, or needs to be Eurocentric. However, given the European imperialism of the last 500 years and how European imperialism has imposed its culture, values, and truth as the "universal," universalism is not exactly a trustworthy idea for some, particularly for postcolonialists.

Globalization as Western Colonization: Postcolonialists

Most critics, particularly on the Left, pinpoint the expansion of predatory capitalism as the main problem of globalization. However, some view globalization as more than (or beyond) the global expansion of capitalism. To them, globalization is a form of Western colonialism, and the continual expansion of Western/European domination (Hardt & Negri, 2000; Harvey, 2003; Amin, 2004). This position shares many of the above critiques of neoliberal global capitalism with World System theories and Marxist theories. Yet, this position, generally called the postcolonialist, regards global race/racism as the core problem of globalization. There may be differences as to why they highlight global race and colonialism in their understanding of globalization. Some do so because they regard race power dynamics as the more fundamental aspect of the current global system. For others, it is because of the constant neglect and marginalization of race by critical theories that they feel the need to put race at its center. Regardless of the reasons, to postcolonialists, the central problem of globalization is global racism. Consequently, the alternatives are to build pedagogies to combat and replace Eurocentric universalism (Leonardo, 2002; Lissovoy, 2008). Recent revived interest in Franz Fanon (Lissovey, 2008; Leonardo & Porter, 2010) is a part of this effort to shed light on racism and postcolonial pedagogy.

While the postcolonialists share the need to overcome Western domination and colonialism, they differ over how to combat global racism and replace Eurocentric domination. Roughly, there are three different trajectories within the post-colonialist position. The first trajectory is what I call the reconstructionist approach. This approach is to reconstruct some of the existing universal principles in line with the globalized world. Their main focus is to remove Eurocentrism from universalism, as we have known it, and to reinvent universalism into more global and universal principles. In other words, these are efforts to reconstruct cosmopolitan consciousness and "universal" universalism from existing modern universalism, be they democracy, human rights, or humanism. Renewed interest in democratic education recently is a good example of this approach (Reid, 2005; Biesta, 2006; Lund & Carr, 2008; Shaker & Heilman, 2008). Others attempt to reconstruct humanism into an approach that is not based on Eurocentrism. For instance, Noah Lissovoy advocates "to discover a new nondominative humanism" in building an alternative education paradigm (Lissovoy, 2008: 5). Similarly, in his call for "a complex critical pedagogy," Joe Kincheloe argues that critical pedagogy needs a new phase. A central task for this new phase of critical pedagogy, according to Kincheloe, is to research subjugated and indigenous knowledges, and to incorporate them into the discipline of critical pedagogy. This incorporation is necessary, according to Kincheloe, in order to "enhance education in general and indigenous/aboriginal education in particular in a multilogical, globalized world" (Kincheloe, 2007: 18).

The second trajectory within the postcolonialist position is the anti-race approach. This approach focuses more explicitly on race, and suggests anti-race and postcolonial pedagogy as the alternative (Leonardo, 2002; Duncan-Andrade & Morrell, 2008). Much inspired by critical race theory, this camp attempts to reposition critical education studies by putting race at their center. Studies of Whiteness and White privilege examine and challenge the Eurocentricity of critical education theories and critical pedagogy. The third trajectory is the indigenous approach. This approach does not see any point in improving or reconstructing Western culture and Eurocentric universalism. In this view there exist fundamental differences and incompatibilities between Western culture and indigenous cultures (see Spring, 2008a). The Western cultural paradigm is individualistic, competitive, instrumental, success-oriented, and rationality-oriented. In contrast, the indigenous culture is based on different views on intellect, relationship, and knowledge. Aboriginal knowledge is personal, oral, experiential, and holistic. Since there are fundamental incompatibilities, they do not see that it is either desirable or feasible to combine the two different cultural values. Therefore, they believe the alternative is not to reconstruct or improve, but rather to replace the hierarchical paradigm of education with indigenous pedagogy (Grande, 2004; Spring, 2007; Villegas et al., 2008). For instance, Joel Spring proposes a new global educational paradigm based on quality of life, instead of education for economic growth and labor market needs. In this new alternative paradigm, Spring continues, "educational policy is focused on longevity and subjective well-being rather than economic success" (Spring, 2007: 2).

Contentions and Implications

In this chapter, I have reviewed alternative visions of education suggested by the globalization studies in education. And I have identified five alternative visions of education: utopian pedagogy, humanist education, localist education alternatives, globalist education alternatives, and postcolonial alternatives. Needless to say, the analyses above are neither exhaustive nor exclusive. There must be other alternative education ideas that are not covered in this chapter. My focus has not been on covering *whose* alternatives, but on figuring out *what* alternatives. We can see that the five alternative visions of education are not mutually exclusive. In fact, some of them can be supportive and complementary of each other. Utopian pedagogy is a broad idea to help us pursue alternative thinking and models, beyond what seems common and feasible. In that way, all the other alternatives can be included within utopian pedagogy. A humanization approach can very well be combined with, and supplementary to the globalist approach, as well as to the localist approach. The need to transform dehumanizing education and the commercialization trend in society is necessary, whether one envisions a global education system or a local system.

Yet, we also see contentions among different alternative trajectories. One contention is the local versus the global. There are those who think the alternative is to develop a local form of schooling (localists), while there are others who think that the way forward is to come up with an alternative global form of schooling (globalists). For localists, diversity and variety are essential and must be protected and enhanced. For globalists, in order to fight against global neoliberalism, we should have some universal goals and global education systems. As we will see in the next chapter, this local/global debate is also a key contention in the search for an alternative society. Another contention is between the universalist and the postcolonialist/indigenous position. One side is trying to come up with some universal principles and values, upon which an alternative education system should be built; be they human rights, humanism, democracy, or individual freedom. However, the other side views these universal values as basically Eurocentrism. Postcolonialists regard Western/modernist thinking as bankrupt, and thus they see that we need to find solutions in indigenous values. In sum, there are differing positions over globalism versus localism, universalism versus particularism/diversity, humanism versus anti-Eurocentrism, and idealism versus materialism. These are some of the issues that critical education has to work through in pursuit of alternative visions of education.

To reiterate, not all alternatives against globalization are coming from critical pedagogy. However, I think there is a considerable overlap between globalization literature and critical pedagogy, in the sense that they both try to find the "language of possibility." As mentioned above, globalization pushes us to come up with alternative paradigms of education, against the neoliberal global movements. Then, what do globalization studies teach critical pedagogy in its pursuit of the "language of possibility"? I believe the five alternatives can help critical pedagogy to clarify and critically examine its own fundamental principles and philosophies. If critical pedagogy considers democracy, human rights, and equality as its guiding values, how would one reconcile the Eurocentric universalism that is embedded in these principles? If one considers critical pedagogy as a fight against the hierarchical and authoritarian power structure, does it deal with the dehumanization, alienation, and fetishism from capitalism? As shown in previous chapters, critical pedagogy has been (and still is) couched largely in moralistic modern philosophies. These moralistic modern principles can be easily co-opted and corrupted by liberalism.

This is why some critics (such as Peter McLaren) have lamented that critical pedagogy had fallen into an easy trap of becoming a "feel-good" pedagogy. In short, the criticism is that critical pedagogy is not critical enough. I believe the critical studies on globalization can help critical pedagogy to be more effectively critical. That said, I do not imply that there have been no serious efforts within critical pedagogy to critically examine its underlying principles. Yet, the globalization education studies have dealt with the universal and modernist Enlightenment principles more forcefully, especially with global perspectives. In addition, anti-globalization studies help us to strengthen the race studies in critical pedagogy. Race has been an important part of critical pedagogy, yet I think that most anti-race pedagogy has limited its discourses to racism within the U.S., or within its nation/country. Globalization studies can help critical pedagogy to extend the multiculturalism and anti-race pedagogy to a global race/racism perspective.

And finally, critical pedagogy has to more explicitly include globalization in its pursuit of alternatives. By looking at the above five visions of alternative education, critical pedagogy has been leaning heavily toward humanism and localism. For one, critical pedagogy has to do more to include the globalization dimension into its traditional foci—in what to teach, how to teach, and how to build a democratic classroom and school culture. In addition, critical pedagogy needs to go beyond the classroom- and pedagogy-focused orientation and has to grapple with the macro-transformation and dynamics of global education movements. It is necessary because globalization is a significant force that has, and will continue to, impact education. And even if one defines critical pedagogy as a matter of "pedagogy," and focuses on transforming pedagogy and classroom culture, one ultimately has to grapple with the larger and fundamental question: what would be the ultimate aims of critical pedagogy? If critical pedagogy is indeed committed to social change, and considers itself as an "agency of change," then it cannot avoid these questions. Ultimately, the questions of critical pedagogy lead us to draw a larger picture of alternative visions of education and society. Are we improving equality (via more equal distribution) within global capitalism? Or are we pursuing a system other than capitalism? Critical education studies on globalization and neoliberal capitalism have provoked many debates and diverse ideas on this very issue. And they will help critical pedagogy to tackle the ultimate and fundamental question: when we talk about schools for "social change," what kind(s) of society are we envisioning? This question, I think, has been largely left unexamined in critical pedagogy. That is the topic for the next chapter.

6

ALTERNATIVE MODELS
OF SOCIETY

Introduction

I still remember vividly the moment when Sandra, a doctoral student of mine, asked the following questions: When we talk about social change, what kind of society are we talking about? What does it look like? Is it beyond capitalism? Shall we get rid of money? When we say we want to get from here to there, what does "there" look like? She wanted to "see" what it would look like. Of course, this was not the first time this question had been raised. I myself wondered about this same question when I was a doctoral student. But somehow, this time, it hit a chord within me. I suddenly remembered *Spaces of Hope* (2000), a book by David Harvey. At the end of the book, Harvey presented a utopian and imaginary society. Since that was the most detailed picture of "there" that I knew of, I gave it to my students, saying "buckle up for a wild ride." However, ever since that day, this question has stayed with me.

This chapter deals with this "there" question. To Freire, an emancipatory education is essential to not only the empowerment of people, but also for them to become subjects of their world. The ultimate aim of emancipatory pedagogy is to change the world through emancipatory education. On this goal, I would say many critical educators are in agreement. And we may agree on some basic principles of this vision, such as equality, justice, democracy, peace, freedom, human rights, and recognition. But what feasible alternatives are we really striving for, or should we strive for? Historically, the Left (not the liberal/progressive/Democratic political movement, as some people have interpreted) has based their alternative visions of society largely on Marxism and socialism, and looked to the Soviet Union and China in the search for alternatives. Now, with the collapse of the Soviet Union and the global expansion of neoliberal capitalism, where do we look for alternatives? What alternative visions/models of society can be imagined against imperialist, neoliberal global capitalism? This is a huge question, and certainly far beyond my ability and knowledge. I am not a sociologist, nor a political scientist, nor an economist. But I feel this book would not be quite complete without at least speculating on the question of "there." Needless to say, my coverage of this enormous topic will necessarily be a cursory one.

Before I move on, one qualification must be offered. There are many studies and theories on the problems with neoliberal globalization, on what issues we ought to tackle and resolve (e.g., the environment, resource wars), and what political courses and directions we should take in this time of transition (e.g., democracy, global justice). There are also diverse theories and groups that present new paradigms as the alternative to global capitalism. We see diverse principles presented as the base for the alternative paradigms: social equity, social justice, social recognition, democracy, cultural empowerment, ecology and bio-equality, humanism, and spiritualism. My review, however, focuses only on alternative *models* of society, particularly against neoliberal global capitalism. In other words, what I am focusing on is what an alternative society looks like. If we are trying to move to someplace else, as Immanuel Wallerstein (1995) puts it, which shore do we want to swim to? This chapter has three parts. The first part presents historical contexts of alternative movements against liberalism in the 20th century. Then, the chapter presents and examines four alternative models to global capitalism. Finally, the chapter discusses some major contentions within these alternative models of society.

The Historical Contexts of Alternative Movements

In order to figure out what alternative societies we ought to pursue, it may be helpful to understand where we have been. Which alternative social systems have we tried in the past? And what have we learned from such past historical alternatives? This section briefly reviews the alternative social systems that emerged in the 20th century. There was a significant shift in our thinking and Left politics around 1968, so I am dividing this historical review with 1968 as a marker. The first section covers the Old Left (1945–1968), and the next section covers the New Left (after 1968).

The Old Left: Three Alternatives (1945–1968)

During 1945–1968, we had three major alternatives: (1) social democracy; (2) socialism; and (3) national liberation movements. To begin with, it is crucial to remember that these movements were alternatives in counter to liberalism, which was the dominant ideology of the modern period, roughly covering the period from the French Revolution (1789) to the fall of Soviet Union in 1989 (Wallerstein, 2004b). Liberalism is used by many, with somewhat different meanings. The definition I use is from David Harvey, which I think captures its core ideas. According to Harvey, liberalism is an "ideology rested upon the idea that free markets, free trade, personal initiative and entrepreneurialism were the best guarantors of individual liberty and freedom and that the 'nanny state' should be dismantled for the benefit of all" (Harvey, 2010: 2).

Laissez-faire capitalism was confronted with a crisis at the beginning of the 20th century, and it soon became clear that the free market could not be self-regulated and there had to be some mechanisms put in place to regulate it. It is in the context of the crisis and limitations of liberalism that we saw three alternatives emerge and become implemented in three different worlds. In the West, welfare state and social democracy emerged as an alternative against the liberal capitalist society. The social-democratic parties (or their similar ones) took to power, at least rotating power, in most of Western Europe, North America, and Australasia. In the East, communist or socialist parties came into power from China and U.S.S.R., to Eastern Europe, constituting about one-third of the world. In the South, national liberation movements came into power in previously colonized countries, in most of Asia, Africa, and the Caribbean, as well as in much of Latin America and the Middle East.

All three alternatives, though they differ in fundamental ways, have at least two commonalities. One, they were all alternative movements to liberalism, to the idea of the free market and individualism. Two, they are similar in that they are all based on the same two-step strategy, which is to first take state power and then, second, to transform society (Wallerstein, 2004b). In other words, the idea is that you have to take political power (the state) in order to change society. To some, this sounds like plain common sense. But, there is another widely held idea that, in order to truly transform society, one has to change the people first, and then the rest of the society will follow.

During 1945–1968, these alternative movements were largely successful in obtaining state power. However, these three alternatives ultimately failed in transforming their societies. Why did they fail at this second step? In the West, since World War II, the one-dimensionality of the marketplace and instrumental rationality has spread into nearly every sphere of life. The emergence of a mass communication and culture industry not only made the cultural sphere a commodity, but also deepened the colonization of the life-world by capital and commodity fetishism. Capitalist relations spread into all facets of life, invading more deeply what were previously believed to be private arenas of life. Thus, while the First World (particularly Northern European countries) was able to set up a welfare state with considerable material benefits to the general population, they failed to transform society fundamentally. Socialism in the East was also not able to make social transformation. The Soviet experiment resulted in rigidity and inefficiency of the system, and a concentration of and monopoly on political power. The nation-building Bandung Project of the Third World also proved a disappointment. Out of the liberation movement rose dictatorships and corrupt national states, as Fanon (1963) had presciently warned against (however, let us not forget that imperial states and multinational corporations were significant contributors to prohibiting the establishment of democratic nation-states in newly decolonized countries). By the 1970s, it became more or less obvious that Third World countries would not be able to catch up to rich nations as modernization theories had led them to believe. Instead, we saw Africa and Latin America falling into economic crisis, plagued with chronic financial instability (debts) and political instability (military coups and the rise of authoritarian regimes) (Herbst, 2000; Saul, 2005). It is within the historical context of the failure of the three alternatives that we must understand why the world erupted in 1968.

1968 Revolutions and The New Left

The worldwide revolutions of 1968 (in Paris, Mexico, and beyond) are a significant marker in Left politics. The 1968 revolutions were protests against U.S. hegemony in the world-system, ignited by the Vietnam War. They were also a rebellion against the three alternatives (discussed above). They were a response to the disappointment of and frustration against the Old Left for its inability to create a welfare state at the world level. The 1968 uprisings were not successful in changing the social systems, but they were crucial in changing social movements. Massimo Teodori (1969) argued that a new political position, which he called the "New Left," developed out of social movements during the 1960s. According to Teodori, there are some core characteristics of the New Left that differentiate it from the Old Left of the 1930s. The most significant shift was a retreat from class-based, anti-capitalism struggles. The international workers' movement was the leading social movement in the 19th century. However, since the late 1930s class-based political movements have been in decline.

The working class in Europe bought into the capitalist system, and the situation was the same, if not worse, in the U.S. The American working class never developed as a strong unified class, and remained fragmented mainly due to geographical mobility, nativism, cultural divisions of the proletariat, and most of all racism (Davis, 1999). Unionism and the momentum for socialism were at their height in the U.S. right after the Great Depression; however, this height was short-lived. By the end of World War II, the labor unions were fully incorporated into the capitalist system. Wartime nationalism, cold war consensus, the economic boom, and the United States' dominance of the world economy inculcated "patriotic, anti-radical and pro-authoritarian attitudes in each generation of workers" (ibid.: 89).

Given the co-optation of the working class into the capitalist system, and the invasion of market logic into private life, the new social movements transitioned from class-based struggles to a broader attack on the system as a totality. It was no longer persuasive to many, even to the Left, to hope that a new social order would improve the human condition, let alone solve social problems. It seemed that fundamental social changes would be neither feasible nor desirable. Rather, it seemed sensible (even if by default) to accept the inevitable immorality of society, in that whatever new social structure was built would likely induce more violence and end up developing into another form of totalitarian authority. The enemy was no longer just capitalism or economic exploitation, but the system as a whole.

Now the struggle has to be at all levels of power. Thus, the 1960s was marked by a rebellion against this conformity to the system/society (Touraine, 1971), and a "critique of the cultural and spiritual deadness ... experienced in American society" (Lerner, 2006: 167). This led the new social movements to focus on the "cultural and psychic fabric" of society.

The incredulity toward systemic changes (mainly the state) marked the beginning of self/identity politics as a new political praxis. As building a moral society fell further out of reach and out of vogue, the focus turned toward the self. John Sanbonmatsu characterizes this change succinctly: "[T]he Sixties had nonetheless effected a shift in tone or style in Western praxis, one that decisively privileged emotive and aesthetic expression of an inner, 'radical' nature over considerations of strategy, theoretical coherence, or the patient construction of a counter-hegemonic movement" (Sanbonmatsu, 2004: 23). From this impetus, we see the burgeoning of identity politics for groups, such as women, minorities, homosexuals, and people with disabilities (Harvey, 1990; Sanbonmatsu, 2004; Tilly, 2004). This self/identity-oriented focus deepened even more as the Left politics and social movements began to decline in the 1970s, and as the New Right became dominant in political and social arenas. We have seen a further withdrawal from social activism and a move toward building "a moral man" (Lerner, 2006).

For the last several decades, liberation struggles have become ever more fragmented, while the search for a common front for such struggles has become a sinful totalizing modernism in disguise, if not an impossibility. We should no longer have illusions about systemic solutions from the top down, we are told; and the only remaining option is grassroots, bottom-up democracy movements. Along with the abandonment of the system (including the state), individual and local struggles have become the main site of social change. It is in this historical context that we have witnessed the recent boom of non-governmental organizations (see Hardt & Negri, 2000), and increased scholarly interest in (and dubious use of) concepts such as social capital, synergy (e.g., Evans, 1996), and the civil society (e.g., Putnam, 1993). John Sanbonmatsu sums it up well:

> Politics will no longer be construed in terms of a struggle for overt political power, nor as a struggle among classes or interests. Instead of dreaming of unitary frameworks and norms, subalterns will root tactical practice in chaos and indeterminacy: dispersed, local disruptions of discursive networks, achieved through the proliferation of identities and what Foucault called subjugated knowledges.
>
> (Sanbonmatsu, 2004: 120)

These new social movements also brought new tactics and strategies. The New Left targets American society as a whole, based on analysis of the total nature of the technocratic system of corporate liberalism. It is "a struggle for a redistribution of power at all levels, and to a different conception of the way in which society should be organized" (Teodori, 1969: 37). From this, direct action and grassroots organization emerged as the essential means of struggle and as the democratic mode of political expression, replacing the strategy of coalition building with liberal and labor forces. Participatory democracy is considered a method capable of guiding and inspiring political action. According to Zeus Leonardo, this might be the impetus that prompted a turn to a meta-theory about process, perhaps best captured by Paulo Freire and Jürgen Habermas' work. I think this is a great insight. Centralized party-led movements of the Old Left were challenged and replaced with spontaneous, decentralized, and grassroots actions and organizations. This anti-organization was partly a product of the 1968 Paris experience, when students were deeply disappointed by the French Communist Party, which sided with the government and called for students to quit the general strike and street uprising and return to the university. The experience of the Communist Party in the Soviet Union did not help either. As communist parties became the establishment, the New Left became deeply skeptical of any centralized organization or leadership.

As such, the New Left embraced decentralized, direct action and grassroots activism as the only viable option. However, this new anti-organization stance was not without problems. For instance, there was a great deal of ambivalence about the leadership of the New Left and, according to Todd Gitlin, this ambivalence, along with "its inability to engender a coherent political ideology and organization," was the main reason for the rapid disintegration of the student movements of the 1960s (Gitlin, 1980: 185). Timothy Brennan (2006) also pointed out that this anti-state stance has been one of the more dangerous political legacies of the late 1970s. Still, the grassroots and decentralized strategies have become a core for the New Left and new social movements. Seen from a strategic point of view, the recent proliferation of nongovernmental organizations (NGOs) is a reflection of this localized political trend against top-down and organizational strategy. NGOs, aptly called "people's organizations," are largely based on bottom-up, grassroots movements critical of, or in opposition to, national states (Petras, 1997; Hardt & Negri, 2000; Sader, 2004). According to *Wikipedia*, there are roughly 40,000 internationally operating NGOs, and even higher numbers of national NGOs

(2 million NGOs each in the U.S. and India), and some 240 NGOs come into existence every year. The vast majority of them were formed in the 1980s and 1990s (Petras & Veltmeyer, 2005). This decentralized and grassroots activism has become a predominant form of social activism, becoming a fundamental principle of groups such as the World Social Forum (Mertes, 2004; Leite, 2005).

In summation, the 1968 revolutions brought a new politics, and left six major consequences, according to Wallerstein. The first consequence is the creation of doubt about the two-step strategy (first, take state power, then transform society). It is no longer assumed that changing hands in state power will result in real transformation of the society. The second is the rejection of the idea of a single-party strategy, that is, "political activity in each state would be most efficacious if channeled through a single party" (Wallerstein, 1995: 214–215). The third is the refusal of the concept that "the only conflict within capitalism that is fundamental is the conflict between capital and labor—and that other conflicts based on gender, race, ethnicity, sexuality, etc. are all secondary, derived, or atavistic" (ibid.: 215). The fourth is doubt about the earlier view that "the idea of democracy is a bourgeois concept that blocks revolutionary activity" (ibid.). Instead, democracy is now viewed as a critical concept for anti-capitalist and revolutionary movements. The fifth is refutation of productivism, which is the idea that productivity has to be increased first in order to transform society to a socialist one. Now, the New Left is critical of the myth of productivism and is more concerned about the negative consequences of productivity ideology, such as ecological crisis, commodification, dehumanization, and the quality of life. The sixth is skepticism about science and scientism—the faith in science as the foundation of the construction of utopia. The idea of progress through science is no longer accepted as a self-evident truth. These new politics of the New Left have brought new anti-systemic movements since 1968.

New Anti-Systemic Movements (since 1968)

Since the 1970s, there have been, according to Wallerstein (2004b), four attempts to develop a better kind of anti-systemic movement, which aims to build a more democratic and egalitarian world: Maoisms, the new social movements, human rights organizations, and anti-globalization movements. While there are some fundamental differences among these four alternative movements, in general they share the characteristics of the New Left politics described above. They place much more attention on the elements of the superstructure (culture), democratic process, and participation of the masses (grassroots). I will briefly review each of these movements.

Maoism was developed during the 1950s and 1960s by Mao Zedong as an alternative communist theory to overcome revisionist Marxism. The basic ideas of Maoism are in line with the characteristics of New Left politics. One central idea of Maoism is "democratic centralism" to enrich the democratic process in the Leninist vanguard party, the mass organizations, and the society (D'Mello, 2009). Also, Maoism takes a different approach to the superstructure, and takes culture much more seriously. Contrary to orthodox Marxism, Maoism believes that "if a conscious effort is made to change the elements of the superstructure, this, in turn, affects the economic base" (ibid.). Another core idea is its position of grassroots mass line ("from the masses, to the masses"). Maoisms were attempted in some of the Third World, such as the Shining Path in Peru, the Naxalites in India, and the Communist Party of Nepal. But, by the end of the 1980s, most of them were severely weakened or destroyed.

The new social movements—the Greens and other environmentalists, the feminists, the campaigns of racial or ethnic minorities—emerged in the 1970s, particularly in Europe. However, by the 1980s, internal divisions and the eventual victory of the reformists over the revolutionaries resulted in the new social movements becoming more like pressure/interest groups. Thus, while new social movements have "more rhetoric about ecology, sexism, racism, or all three," they all became more like social democratic (Wallerstein, 2004b: 268). The human rights organizations claimed to speak for "civil society." Yet they, too, soon changed into NGOs, and have become "more like the adjuncts of states than their opponents, and, on the whole, scarcely seem very antisystemic" (ibid.: 269).

Finally, the anti-globalization movements, too, have seen a notable rise in recent years. They are protests and fights against the social ills consequent of neoliberalism, and they encompass all types of groups across the ideological spectrum, although NGOs are the most visible within the anti-globalization movements. The best example of anti-globalization movements is the World Social Forum (WSF). WSF, which was formed in 2001 in Porto Alegre, Brazil, is the antithesis of the World Economic Forum in Davos. It is the first global platform for discussing strategies of resistance to neoliberal globalization. It has daringly proclaimed that "Another World is Possible" as its slogan. Although WSF replaced the term "anti-globalization" with "global justice" in 2002 (Moraff, 2009), the main problem with WSF and the anti-globalization movements is that they have no clear ideological footing, no clear strategy, and no clear programs. As such, it is unclear whether anti-globalization movements can become, or present, a real alternative. All in all, these four recent anti-systemic movements have either been destroyed, weakened, co-opted, or are in disarray.

Alternative Models to Global Capitalism

While Left politics and social movements have transformed, the conditions of the world economy have also changed. After the 1968 revolutions, the world plunged into another economic crisis in 1973 (oil crisis). What we have witnessed since the 1970s is the unfolding of a structural crisis in capitalism. Many scholars suggest that we are in a transition period (Wallerstein, 1995; Hardt & Negri, 2000; Hobsbawm, 2009; Harvey, 2010). This is the end of an era, and, as such, a time of turbulence and reactionary politics. Heightened ethnic/religious/cultural conflicts are symptoms of this crisis, as well as the recent surge of U.S. militarism. In essence, neoliberalism is also a reaction to this larger structural crisis and transition. Neoliberalism is reviving liberalism to reconstruct the dominant ideology (thus, "neo" liberalism). Within this economic crisis and global polarization, and in this time of transition, the question to ask is: what alternative models/visions of society do we have, or think we have, against the neoliberal global capitalism? There are diverse ideas, theories, and approaches to this large question. In the following, I present only four alternative models of society: (1) reformists: social democracy with welfare state; (2) globalists: global socialism and supernational politics; (3) localists: autarchy and earth democracy; and (4) mixed economy of public and private.

Reformists: Social Democracy with Welfare State

One alternative to neoliberal global capitalism is to reform capitalism: to improve the welfare state and social democracy, and to expand it to a global scale. In existing capitalism, there are variations, from liberal capitalism to welfare capitalism, from laissez-faire capitalism to state capitalism. In a way, this approach aims to find a better form of capitalism, or improve capitalism with more equal distribution. As such, the focus of this approach is on the distribution side: the equal distribution of wealth, the social protection for the disadvantaged, and the equal (or less unequal) global distribution of wealth and resources. This position does not attempt to change production (private ownership of property and production for profit). The reasons for not dealing with production may vary: changing the capitalist production system is less feasible, or the change of production is too chaotic or costly, or capitalist production is the most efficient system. Whatever the reasons, this position seeks to find a solution within the capitalist system.

The basis of social democracy and welfare capitalism is that of compensation for the inequalities and social ills that liberal capitalism inevitably has created. The state intervenes and regulates the market, and provides protection for the disadvantaged. Social democracy and the welfare state stabilized the market by limiting crisis and improving the living standards for the general public. As stated above, social democracy and welfare capitalism was experimented within the industrialized West after World War II. The best examples of social democratic welfare capitalism are found in the Scandinavian and Northern European countries, such as Sweden, Norway, Finland, and the Netherlands.

I think this is a widely held position among progressives and Leftists. In fact, this has been the position of labor in the West since the 1950s (Hobsbawm, 2009). Rather than demanding a change of the economic production system (i.e., revolution), labor and the labor union in the industrialized nations consented to achieve more equal distribution of wealth. Looking historically, this position has become particularly appealing and popular, especially since the 1980s. Roughly speaking, the Left looked to the socialism of Russia and China in the 1950s and 1960s. However, once authoritarianism and rigidity arose and became clear in the socialist blocs, the Left turned to the national development of Latin America and began to see dependency theories as a way forward. However, as the Latin American economy started to suffer in the late 1970s, the Left began to have second thoughts about the promise of the dependency theory. After the downfall of Latin American development and socialist blocs, we have seen the erosion of the dependency theory and socialist theories. Then, the social democracy of Northern Europe seemed to hold merit to many.

The key problem with this position, however, is whether it is possible to expand welfare capitalism to the global scale. Welfare capitalism in the North was possible due to the existence of the South. The enhancement of the living standards of the industrialized nations since the 1960s was based on the exploitation of the underdeveloped countries. The South provided cheap materials to the North, which was essential for the industrialization of the North ("primary accumulation"). Also, the underdeveloped countries have been important markets for the manufactured goods from the First World. This unequal trade gave advantages to the North and made its welfare capitalism possible. But the underdeveloped countries do not have their

"South" to help their own development. In other words, the underdeveloped or undeveloped countries have to transform themselves into welfare capitalist states without the advantage of primary accumulation.

Some argue that this transformation is still possible without the existence of primary accumulation, because of the globalization and technical advancement we now have. However, the trade inequalities still persist between the industrialized countries and less industrialized countries. Furthermore, due to the rise of neoliberalism in recent decades, social democracy based on a welfare state has been in retreat. In fact, neoliberalism is an attack (renewed) on the welfare state and social democracy. With the serious financial crisis we are in now, it is not clear how appealing and successful this alternative can be. And yet, I believe many progressives and critical educators favor reforming capitalism, holding to their principles and values such as equality, justice, democracy, inclusion, diversity, and freedom. Or perhaps some do not believe in the idea of capitalism, yet they take this position because they think reforming capitalism may be the only feasible option we have.

Globalists: Global Socialism and Supernational Politics

To some, global capitalism is beyond reforming or fixing, and thus the only alternative is to abolish global capitalism and to replace it with another global system. In other words, this position is not anti-globalization, but counter-globalization. Among the globalists, the most apparent idea is global socialism. Although many in the Left have distanced themselves from socialism/communism since the late 1980s, some still believe that socialism is the solution and the direction we should move toward. In a speech given at the *World Social Forum 2010* at Porto Alegre, David Harvey (2010) passionately argued, "[I]f, as the alternative globalization movement of the late 1990s declared, 'another world is possible' then why not also say 'another communism is possible'?" Here, it needs to be pointed out that the socialism Harvey and others advocate is not the same kind of socialism as the central, state-planned economies of the Soviet model. In fact, Harvey (ibid.) states that recent attempts to revive socialism/communism typically reject state control, and seek other forms of collective social organization. The desired form of communism, according to Harvey, is "[h]orizontally networked as opposed to hierarchically commanded systems of producers and consumers."

I will focus on Samir Amin (1997) to illustrate major points of the global socialist position. Unlike localists (to be reviewed in the next section), Amin does not believe that separation and localism is an alternative to global capitalism. Instead, he accepts globalization as an inevitable and desirable trend. As an alternative to neoliberal global capitalism, Amin advocates "polycentric regionalization" as a step toward eventual global socialism. According to Amin (and others, such as Habermas, Wallerstein, and Harvey), the world has been in structural crisis since the early 1970s. This crisis is due to two factors, says Amin. One factor is the internal contradictions, limitations inherent in class relations in a social-democratic compromise, and ambitions of the Soviet bourgeois and those of the Third World. The second is the everlasting globalization of capitalism, which creates polarization. As a result, we see the erosion of the nation-state, the erosion of the great divide between the industrialized center and non-industrialized periphery, and the emergence of new dimensions of polarization. The neoliberalism that has developed since the 1980s, according to Amin, is a reaction to the globalization of capital—especially the globalization of financial capital. Globalization of financial capital is characterized by a cessation of investment in productive/industrial capital, liberalization of international capital movements, floating exchange rates, high rates of interest, Third-World debt, and privatization.

To this structural crisis, global socialism is the ultimate solution, according to Amin. But as a way toward global socialism, he advocates "coherent delinking" to fight off global capital and the global dominance of the U.S. (he is one of the original "dependency theorists"), and establishing a polycentric world system on both the economic and the political levels. Based on that idea, Amin proposes radical reforms of global and international institutions and structures. Some of his propositions are: reform of the WTO for planning access to the use of the major natural resources of the globe and the price of raw materials, regulating trades favoring the disadvantaged regions, channeling excess finance/savings toward productive investment in the peripheries, reform of the international monetary system into regional monetary systems to guarantee relative stability of exchange rates, transforming the IMF into a world central bank, democratization of the United Nations, adaptation of citizenship income instead of wage, world taxation, and establishment of a world parliament (Amin, 1997).

There are other globalists who advocate a different globalism. For instance, Jürgen Habermas (2001) is in agreement with Amin (and others) in that the economy is globalized and the nation-state era is over. However, the real problem, according to Habermas, is the discord between the globalized economy and politics, which is still based on the nation-state. In other words, politics are not catching up to the globalized economy.

Thus, the urgent issue confronting us, Habermas argues, is to globalize politics. Thus, the key question we are facing and need to resolve is "whether the civil society and the political public sphere of increasingly large regimes can foster the consciousness of an obligatory cosmopolitan solidarity" (ibid.: 55). Therefore, what Habermas calls the "supernational politics" should be based on global citizens instead of national citizens, and should formulate cosmopolitan consciousness instead of nationalism. While Habermas is for the idea of global political governance, he is against establishing a global government, as in the organizational form of a world state. Instead, what Habermas envisions as an alternative is a loosely developed global governance structure that gives maximum freedom for local governance, where diversity and differences will flourish, and where "the autonomy, particularity, and uniqueness of formerly sovereign states will have to be taken into account" (ibid.: 56). Given that, the focus of Habermas' project is not on reforming governments. Rather, Habermas argues that "the first addresses for this 'project' are not governments. Rather, they are social movements and non-governmental organizations; the active members of a civil society that stretches beyond national borders" (ibid.). This may seem somewhat ambiguous, but Habermas sees the European Union as an example in this direction, and a significant historical experiment for the future.

Among the globalists, there are economic globalists (such as Samir Amin), and political globalists (such as Jürgen Habermas). However, they share the common idea that the alternative system against neoliberal global capitalism has to be a global one. The key problem with a globalist approach would be feasibility. Given the imbalance of power among nations, and the enormous wealth gap between the rich and the poor countries, some may see any global model as almost impossible to establish. Another problem or critique of the globalists is the issue of universalism (which I will elaborate on later). The issue is whether and how to come up with a global model that is acceptable to all. And even so, the issue is whether a global system results in imposing one's values to others.

Localists: Autarchy and Earth Democracy

The proponents of this position do not believe in fixing or improving the existing global capitalism, because they think global capitalism is beyond repair. Since capitalism is based on profits-based production, and as long as profits are the motive for production, they see that capitalism will continue to create exploitation and inequalities. The localists agree with the globalists in that global capitalism has to be dismantled and replaced, rather than being improved or fixed. However, they do not believe in replacing it with another global social system either (such as global socialism). Instead, they believe that localization is the way to survive and fight against global capitalism that threatens and destroys lives, especially in the Third World. In short, this is basically an anti-globalization, anti-capitalism position.

Maria Mies (1986) is a good example of advocates of localist alternative. According to Mies, an alternative social system to global capitalism is a self-sufficient economic system. This autarchy economy is self-sufficient with small-scale, decentralized farms. In contrast to orthodox Marxist economic theory, Mies considers the capitalist production process as the super-exploitation of non-wage laborers (women, colonies, and peasants) upon which wage labor exploitation is then possible.

Mies argues that the general production of life, or subsistence production, constitutes the perennial basis upon which capitalist productive labor can be built up and exploited (this was the main point of Rosa Luxemburg). Therefore, Mies claims that there are underground connections among:

1. men's exploitation and domination of nature;
2. women's subordination in Europe; and
3. the conquest and colonization of other lands and people.

These three problems are not separate, but they are all linked as essential elements of capitalism. Therefore, the solution, according to Mies, should be in changing the mode of production. The alternative system should be based on production of goods for use (not for exchange) and production for life (not for profit).

Vandana Shiva (2005) adds eco-democracy into the localist approach. Shiva is similar to Mies, in that she argues that production should be for use, not for exchange, and for life, not for profit. However, her idea of production-for-life extends beyond human beings. She extends life to humans, animals, plants, and to all life on earth. Based on her activist work in India and other countries, Shiva calls for "earth democracy" as a solution, which is both an ancient worldview and an emergent political movement for peace, justice, and sustainability. Earth democracy, she proclaims, is "to claim our common humanity and our unity with all life" (ibid.: 8). Shiva not only adds ecology and resource democracy to the localist approach, but she also views the resource conflicts and ecology as the source of global conflicts. According to Shiva, the ecology movement is not just about protection of the environment. She maintains that environmental issues are related to conflicts, democracy, peace, and security. A core issue of the environment should be global-level resource wars. Shiva maintains, "[i]n the Third World, ecology movements are not a luxury of the rich: they are a survival imperative for the majority of people whose life is put at risk by the market economy and threatened by its expansion" (ibid.: 49). Thus, Shiva argues that terrorism and the rise of fundamentalism are due to the unequal distribution of resources, not due to religious differences or cultural clashes. Furthermore, Shiva emphasizes that the choice between a global or local approach is a false dichotomy, saying that "[e]arth democracy connects the particular to the universal, the diverse to the common, and the local to the global" (ibid.: 1). Yet, she seems to put more emphasis on local democracy, saying that "only on the foundations of strong local democracy can strong national and global democracies be built" (ibid.: 84). In that sense, Shiva is more of a "glo-cal" advocate.

In sum, the localist approach is based on the belief that the needs of locales could be best met by the local economy. Also, it views diversities and differences as invaluable elements, not to be sacrificed by common or global ideas. Furthermore, some localists—although not all—criticize capitalism by fundamentally challenging and rejecting the model of production for exchange-value and profits. In that sense, I think that they are more radical than the others (e.g., global socialists).

Mixed Economy of Public and Private

Above, I presented three alternative models to global capitalism: The first is to reform global capitalism, the second is to replace it with global socialism, and the third is to replace it with a local economic system for subsistence production. However, there are others who do not believe in capitalism, or socialism, or autarchy as the alternative for the future. This position aims to come up with a new kind of system. There are various ideas within this position, but I will focus on the mixed economy idea by Eric Hobsbawm (2009). Hobsbawm claims that both socialism and capitalism have failed, and argues that the future lies in a kind of mixed economy of public and private. But it has to be noted that Hobsbawm is not talking about "theories" of socialism or capitalism. He is referring the "existing" (real) socialism and capitalism that were experimented with in the 20th century.

According to Hobsbawm, what we have attempted to realize so far were socialism and capitalism in "their pure form." One was the centrally state-planned economies of the Soviet type, and the other was the totally unrestricted and uncontrolled free-market capitalist economy. These two models have disappeared in history, and are no longer feasible. Soviet-type socialism broke down in the 1980s, and free-market capitalism is breaking down right now. Hobsbawm maintains that the present world crisis is the greatest crisis of global capitalism ever, and it marks the end of free-market capitalism. He argues that we need to change the dominant ideology of "maximum economic growth and commercial competitiveness," which has been the basis not only for capitalism, but also for socialism. Therefore, the alternative for the future, according to Hobsbawm, is "mixed economies in which public and private are braided together in one way or another." How to braid the public and private—that is our task to figure out. But as a guiding principle for the mixed economy, Hobsbawm presents "public decisions aimed at collective social improvement." This means, according to him, a move away from the free market to public, non-profit initiative.

There must be others who advocate a similar approach. For instance, Bowles and Gintis (2001) also advocate this position. Bowles and Gintis envision "a system of democratically-run and employee-owned enterprises coordinated by both markets and governmental policies" (ibid.: 21), as a better alternative to capitalism. The mixed economy approach has some similarities and overlaps with other approaches. It takes the same position with the localists, in challenging and rejecting the dominant premise of private wealth and consumption. The idea of combining the private and public economy could be more acceptable to some people. Maybe it is because this approach looks more feasible than others, as it does not seem to require a radical transformation, such as a total abolishment of the private market. If understood this way, the mixed system of private and public looks to be the same approach as welfare capitalism and social democracy. However, as far as Eric Hobsbawm is concerned, the mixed economy model is neither capitalism nor socialism. And he believes that we do not yet know how to combine the public and the private.

Contentions and Issues

Among the four models I reviewed above, only the first one attempts to find a solution within capitalism. The rest aim to replace capitalism, while they differ in terms of with what. I am sure that there are other approaches that I have failed to include. Also, some ideas may overlap or occupy in-between positions. As limited as the reviews above are, we can see some fundamental and important contentions within these alternative models. I will highlight four major contentions/issues. These contentions are basically the same as the contentions in alternative models of education against globalization, as reviewed in Chapter 5.

The first is a contention between the local and the global. At one end of the spectrum, there is the idea that the only alternative to global capitalism is to go local—to develop a self-sufficient economic system oriented to sustainability (autarchy). At the other end of the spectrum, the claim is not to reject globalization, but to develop a different kind of global system (such as global socialism). As seen in the previous chapter, this local/global divide is reflected in critical education and its alternative models of education.

The second is the tension between the state and civil society. While one side still believes that the target of change is to transform the state, the other side does not believe in the power of the state, and promotes change and reformation of "civil society." This different position is significant, as it affects the form and organization of social movements. The state-centered side is more likely to prioritize a party-led, organized, and centralized struggle. The civil society-oriented side relies more on spontaneous, grassroots movements, which are decentralized, non-hierarchical, and adopt dispersed forms and tactics. In other words, the civil society orientation is a localized, bottom-up approach, and it tends to be critical or skeptical of the state and top-down solutions. Currently, the position of the bottom-up approach and civil society seems to be the most popular among feminists and social activists. The original idea of NGOs stemmed from this position, although in reality NGOs and NP (non-profit) entities have been incorporated into, and thus come to play complementary roles to, the capitalism system (Tang, 2005).

The third is a contention over power. One of the crucial debates in the new social movements is about power (i.e., whether to take power—meaning, state power—or not). Since John Holloway (2002) published *Change the World Without Taking Power*, there have been serious and spirited debates regarding how new social movements should promote social change. While Holloway promotes a local and grassroots approach without taking power, there are others who have great concerns about such a localized, grassroots direction for social movements. For instance, Phil Hearse (2007) criticizes Holloway's approach, arguing that we need to *Take the Power to Change the World*.

Finally, the fourth is the tension between universalism and particularism. The new social movements are geared to particularistic politics, such as identity politics and single-issue oriented movements. These are, as stated before, a protest against universalism. Others see the politics of differences as fragmented, and argue that we need to search for politics and movements based on some universalism. Again, we saw this same contention in critical education. So, instead of repeating it, I want to add some theoretical debates on this issue. The issue of universalism (or the universal truth) has been the key issue in social philosophy and epistemology. In fact, these are the opposing positions between German philosophers (such as Habermas), and the French poststructuralists (such as Foucault, and Lyotard). Habermas (2001) asks: where do we go after the death of the truth (heralded by Immanuel Kant)? He speculates that there are basically three options: relativism, local determinism, or diversity/multicultural differences. He does not agree with the French postmodernist position, which claims the death of grand theories and resorts to local narratives (Lyotard is the one he is specifically referring to). To Habermas, the question is: how can we salvage something from universalism without totalitarian and colonial tendencies/dangers? As is well known, he tries to find an answer via communicative action and rationality. Wallerstein is similar to Habermas in believing that it is possible to come up with some universalisms. Wallerstein declares that the era of European universalism has ended, and one possible alternative is "a multiplicity of universalisms that would resemble a network of universal universalisms" (Wallerstein, 2006: 84).

Implications for Critical Pedagogy

As I finish this review of the alternative models of society, I realize again how enormous this topic is and how limited my analysis is. Even with such limitation, I have tried to present some thoeries on alternative forms of society. In closing, I will briefly mention some of the implications we can draw from the above review of alternative social systems. One thing to notice is that the politics of critical pedagogy are very much in alignment with the politics of the new social movements and the New Left. We see that critical pedagogy shares the same strategies and political stances with the New Left—such as a great attention to culture, an emphasis on identity and multiplicity, a focus on individual transformation rather than system changes, a preference to localism, a distrust toward the state and a leaning toward the civil society, a strong emphasis on the participatory/grassroots democracy, and a principle of an anti-authority structure. The review in this chapter, I hope, helps us to better understand the general political stances of critical pedagogy.

The other thing is, as seen above, the contentions and issues are almost same for alternative education and alternative society.

In both, we see the same contentions between localism and the globalism, and between universalism and particularism. This, of course, makes sense, as critical education theories are a sub-field of critical social theories, and thus are influenced by, or in sync with the same theories and issues belonging to larger social theories. Also, critical educators can learn from the critiques raised on productivism/developmentalism, from skepticism and critiques on science, and from reconsiderations of democracy. I think it will help us if we take these issues more seriously in our pursuit of alternative education.

In closing, a critical pedagogue's idea may not fit in one model or approach for alternative models of society. He/she may not need to choose one model. Needless to say, social change does not exactly happen as we intend or envision. Furthermore, I think educators have only limited power or roles to play for social change. However, as long as we proclaim that critical pedagogy (and critical education) strives to be an agent of social change, I think it would be helpful to at least brood over what kind of society we are pursuing and imagining. It is particularly so, because I think it is easy to forget this question while we are busy with details of education. Therefore, it is important to keep it in mind, and keep thinking about this big question. At the end of the day, "there" is the most important question for critical educators—to where we want to be heading.

7

CONCLUSION

I am talking about something that's so impossible, it can't possibly be true. But it's the only way the world's gonna survive, this impossible thing. My job is to change five billion people to something else. Totally impossible. But everything that's possible's been done by man, I have to deal with the impossible. And when I deal with the impossible and am successful, it makes me feel good because I know that I'm not bullshittin'.

(Sun Ra, in Szwed, 1997: 295)

Limitations of the Change Agent

This book, thus far, has been a systematic analysis of critical pedagogy. The focus of this book has been to evaluate competing theories of the "language of possibility," to critically examine the alternative projects of critical pedagogy, and to present directions for better alternative education. Although critical pedagogy claims to impact and change society, I have argued that there are inherent limitations within the dominant discourses of critical pedagogy that stifle the possibility of social change. For this reason, I have argued that critical pedagogy, as it is, will at best modernize, rather than change society. I will briefly recap the main tendencies within critical pedagogy, which limit its efforts to search for the "language of possibility." The limitations and tendencies below are not unique to critical pedagogy. I believe some of these limitations can be found in critical education in general.

The first concern is critical pedagogy's tendency toward de-politicization. Critical pedagogy is a broad field with varying ideas, sometimes too diverse to the point of confusion. We need to clarify just what critical pedagogy is, particularly because there is a de-politicized version/view of it. As Freirean pedagogy has often utilized a de-politicized technique of teaching, there is a tendency to understand critical pedagogy as merely a teaching method. If I had to choose the most important concept of critical pedagogy, it would be power. Of course, power is a complicated concept, and there are many different approaches to/conceptions of power. However, if one does not understand power, or does not include the complex dynamics of power in one's understanding and analysis of critical pedagogy, then while one may be talking about a "good" pedagogy, it cannot be about critical pedagogy. This rather simple fact—that critical pedagogy is essentially a political project and, thus, essentially about power—is surprisingly less than obvious to some. While I am not suggesting that all critical pedagogies are de-politicized, yet I advocate the re-emphasis and reinsertion of the political element into critical pedagogy.

The second concern, closely related to the first, is a liberal/ reformist tendency within critical pedagogy, especially as it relates to what we are ultimately trying to achieve. In critical pedagogy, we bandy about concepts such as social change, social transformation, emancipation, liberation, democracy, equality, diversity, and social justice. Recently, these ideas have been so contaminated by the Right (for instance, a claim that we make war to make peace) and commercialized by market economy (diversity and social change as marketing strategy) that it is hard to take them at face value. Setting this contamination issue aside, these are abstract ideas that can be interpreted in many ways (liberally, radically, and everything in-between). From my experience, I think there is somewhat of a liberal lean in critical pedagogy. From this perspective, critical pedagogy is about sharing power, reducing discrimination, and achieving equality/equal opportunity. In other words, the target is usually the people who have power, rather than the power structure itself. As such, the goal of critical pedagogy has been to fix or improve the system, instead of dismantling it.

The third concern is moralism. By moralism, I mean that there is a tendency to understand critical pedagogy as a moral project (doing the right thing). In other words, the core issues of education (as well as the society at large) are understood and defined as moral/ethical problems. Critical pedagogy has become, essentially, a moralizing project, or more specifically, about moralizing individuals. This is a somewhat tricky issue. Of course, as critical pedagogy is a political project, it inevitably involves morality. However, there is a difference between being moral and being moralistic. There is an assumption (sometimes hidden and sometimes not so hidden) that critical pedagogy is better than other pedagogies, and similarly, that critical pedagogues are somehow better than and more enlightened as compared to other pedagogues (the unenlightened ones), and that the job of critical pedagogy is to enlighten the rest of the unenlightened. Of course, critical pedagogy (and teaching in general) involves conscientization (as Freire demonstrates); yet, fixating on individuals for moral transformation is a limited, dangerous project. That said, it needs to be noted that the moralizing (modernist) approach has been much criticized and challenged within critical pedagogy. Particularly, feminists from poststructuralism and postmodernism have tried to present "genuinely" critical and power-free pedagogy, beyond the dualist modernist epistemology and moralism, by employing the Nietzschean position of non-dualism ("beyond good and evil"). Yet, I do not think these challenges have made any real impact on critical pedagogy. The reason seems simple. It is because, in the end, they too have been unable to articulate what this "non-dualistic critical pedagogy" is (or should be).

The fourth concern revolves around culture and post-modernism. Initially, I thought the problem was simply an overabundance of culturalism and postmodernism within critical pedagogy. However, the real problem, I believe, is not too much culture and postmodernism, but rather their mis-understanding and misuse. Many concepts have been too easily borrowed from poststructuralism and postmodernism, and transposed to critical pedagogy. New terminologies have been widely circulated, including technologies of power, the regime of truth, subjugated knowledges, and grand/meta-narratives. The problem is, however, not with these new concepts and terminologies. The real problem is, I believe, that these powerful yet complex concepts and theories are too often misunderstood and applied superficially. So in the end, contrary to its claim, critical pedagogy has been unable to incorporate these powerful ideas from postmodernism.

The fifth concern is the focus on the micro-level (focus on individuals, classrooms, and teaching), where educators supposedly have direct impact. Again, I am not suggesting that critical pedagogues have only promoted micro-centered pedagogy and politics. I believe that many critical pedagogues are not only aware of the extant systematic problems, but also desire more fundamental changes to the system. However, critical educators are overwhelmed by the amount of work required for such systematic change. How do we change the system? Is it feasible to abolish capitalism? This all seems simply too much for them to even begin to imagine. Thus, critical pedagogy has concentrated on schools and classrooms, and has tried to effect change there. This micro-approach seems to concentrate the "language of possibility" on the process (how to practice critical pedagogy). In its emphasis on the process, the process itself becomes the goal of alternatives. In other words, a micro-level focus loses track of the prize. To me, the prize is social change, however one defines it.

The sixth concern is localism. Critical pedagogy tends to be underpinned by localist/particularist politics. There are historical reasons/contexts as to why and how we have arrived at localist politics. The new sensibility to local democracy is a corrective response to previous Leninist politics. However, it would be unfortunate if localist politics limited or narrowed our attention exclusively to individualistic or localized concerns. Furthermore, localist/particularist politics can be powerless or even dangerous, if neoliberal capitalism is successful in weakening the public (including the state). There is yet much about the public and the state that can and should be defended. Although critical educators may eagerly embrace the popular mantra, "Think globally, act locally," I argue that critical pedagogy is actually quite weak at thinking globally. This is an opportune time for critical pedagogists to take globalism seriously, and to re-conceptualize and re-explore what Immanuel Wallerstein has called the "universal universalisms," which go beyond Euro-centric universalism (Wallerstein, 2006: 84). Or, as Habermas (2001) puts it, we are in great need of development of a "post-national" cosmopolitan consciousness.

Finally, the seventh concern is critical pedagogy's specula-tive and idealistic tendencies in its pursuit for alternatives. By idealism, I do not mean utopianism or the search for an idealistic situation. Rather, what I mean by idealism is the un-materialistic, in contrast to realism/materialism. The dis-course of critical pedagogy is couched in abstract and ethical ideals such as hope, love, democracy, utopia, and care. Recently, we have seen an outpouring of literature based on these ideals. These are beautiful ideas, which are hard to oppose. However, I think this tendency of idealism is quite problematic. When critical pedagogy concentrates on ideals without presenting concrete pragmatic projects, it can become idealistic, even speculative. This is what Gramsci has called the "speculative" distortion of theory, which happens when knowledge is pro-duced without direct link to or use in reality. I am not suggest-ing that critical pedagogy, as a whole, is based on speculative politics. What I am suggesting, however, is that in order to realize the promises of critical pedagogy, we need to guard against critical pedagogy succumbing to its speculative and idealistic tendencies.

A Sketch for Future Direction

How can schools become agents of social change? Liberal pluralism (the mainstream ideology of capitalism) postulates that the only possibility is to modernize the system through the promotion of equal rights and the elimination of discrimination. With increasingly intensifying globalization, what we are told by the mainstream education paradigm is that schools must educate students better, so that our nation/economy can compete better in the increasingly competitive global market. After all, we are told, education is about individual students, so let us focus on meeting their needs and educating our students as best as we can. The idea of social change via schools may be a desirable ideal, but it is nothing more than just an ideal, an illusion. What we need to do is to improve what we have. That is what liberal pluralism tells us.

So, what could and should schools do? I think it may be helpful to approach alternative education in terms of "multi-level" strategies. Immanuel Wallerstein (2004a) believes that the modern era has ended, and we are in times of transition. And in such times of transition, Wallerstein suggests that we need to develop strategies with multiple components. His suggestion is specifically targeted for the World Social Forum, but I think it can be useful for our search for alternative visions of education. The first component that Wallerstein recommends is to maintain a process of constant and open debate about the transition and the outcomes we are hoping for. Critical education and critical pedagogy have certainly been engaged in such debates for at least the past three decades. And it is my hope that this book can contribute to furthering and revitalizing our debates on alternative visions of education.

The second component is to set up short-term defensive actions. In this, Wallerstein emphasizes that the defensive actions are "not to remedy the system, but to prevent its negative effects from getting worse in the short run" (Wallerstein, 2004b: 272). We can set up some defense actions against neoliberal educational reforms, and there have already been some actions on this front (for example, *Education for All*). The agendas of what I call the liberal version of critical pedagogy could be employed as defensive actions, as long as we are clear that they are only temporary, defensive actions. We can utilize these tactics to minimize the negative consequences of marketization and privatization of neoliberal education reforms. It is easier said than done, but we should not forget that these actions are not meant to fix or maintain the system.

The third component is to establish interim, middle-range goals that move in the right direction. Specifically, the right direction, according to Wallerstein, is moving toward selective, but ever-widening, decommodification. Finally, the fourth component is to develop long-term emphases/goals. To that effect, Wallerstein suggests "a relatively democratic and relatively egalitarian world" (ibid.: 272–273). Decommodification and a more democratic and egalitarian world, it seems to me, are certainly the right mid- and long-term goals/directions for alternative education. As we have reviewed in previous chapters, there have been efforts to propose mid- and long-term goals for alternative education, particularly against the neoliberal global educational reforms: utopian pedagogy, humanist education, localist pedagogy, eco-pedagogy, post-colonial pedagogy, and indigenous pedagogy.

For setting our mid- and long-term goals for alternative visions of education, one thing that is absolutely necessary is to challenge and re-examine Enlightenment modernism and liberalism, or "the regime of truth" of our modern era. Foucault (1980) identifies five traits of the regime of truth in modern Western societies:

1. "truth" is centered on the form of scientific discourse and the institutions which produce it;
2. "truth" is subject to constant economic and political incitement;
3. "truth" is the object, in diverse forms, of immense diffusion and consumption;
4. "truth" is produced and transmitted under the dominant (if not exclusive) control of a few political and economic apparatuses; and
5. "truth" is the nexus of a larger political debate and social confrontation (i.e., "ideological struggle").

The essential political problem for the intellectual, Foucault argues, is "detaching the power of truth from the forms of hegemony, social, economic and cultural, within which it operates at the present time" (ibid.: 133). If Foucault got these traits of the regime of truth of our time right (and I would argue that he did), then what that means, among other things, is that we cannot build long-term goals for alternative education *without* detaching the economic link to knowledge and *without* challenging scientific discourse. And I must add that we have, indeed, been challenging the regime of truth, particularly the economic link and the science discourse (and I think this is, in a nutshell, what poststructuralism and postmodernism is about).

However, I think there are missing elements in Foucault's traits of the modern regime of truth, namely nationalism and

Eurocentrism. I believe that nationalism and Eurocentrism are essential traits of the modern regime of truth. And I argue that, in our visions of alternative education, we need to include nationalism and Eurocentrism. As such, I believe that, in setting our mid- and long-term goals for alternative education, we must consider the following key issues/topics. First is the topic of the nation-state. Modern school systems have been built as nation-state projects. However, with globalization, we now need to explore how to redefine the link between modern school systems and the nation-state. The modern education system, thus far, has largely constructed and promoted national consciousness. However, it is now crucial for critical education to find a way to transform national consciousness into global and transnational consciousness. Another related issue for critical education is Eurocentrism, or Eurocentric universalism. By now, we are aware of the fundamental problems and limitations with modernism, and European universalism. Some even argue that we are witnessing the end of European universalism (Wallerstein, 2004a), or a crisis of Western thinking (Foucault, 1999). As we are witnessing the end of the modern era and increasing globalization, we have to find a way to overcome European universalism and global racism, and to construct a "universal" universalism.

Education as a Change Agent

So, now back to the original question: *can* critical pedagogy really be a change agent? Better yet, *how* can education be a change agent? Paradoxically, because of its initial claim to be a "language of possibility," critical pedagogy has ended up focusing on mainly what is feasible and possible. Previous critical education theories (Marxist, neo-Marxist, and structural theories) have pointed out that the social structure/system (mostly capitalism) is the root of educational problems. Logically, the ultimate solution, according to these theories, would be a total, or a fundamental change of the social system (i.e., abolishment of capitalism or something similar). It is not hard to see why this kind of structural transformation would seem unfeasible, unimaginable, or undesirable to many, even to some critical educators. I think "there is no alternative" syndrome runs deep in our mind, perhaps deeper than critical educators realize (perhaps, this "impossibility" is the biggest hegemony of our time in the U.S.). Hence, critical pedagogy has turned and gone to the possible, the imaginable, the thinkable, and the feasible, in order to find a "language of possibility." Therefore, critical pedagogy has ended up focusing on the micro-level where, seemingly, educators can do *something*.

Critical education theories featured strong structural analysis in the 1970s with Bowles and Gintis. Due to the limitations of their theory (and, more importantly, due to changes in capitalism), critical education, particularly critical pedagogy, has moved away not only from Bowles and Gintis, but also from structural analysis itself. However, I think we have moved too far away. We may not need to return exactly to Bowles and Gintis (although I believe that they had it right), but critical pedagogy can benefit from including a structural/macro-analysis into its micro-oriented perspective. That is why I have endeavored to turn the lens of analysis to a more macro-perspective, by attempting to re-insert micro-developments within critical pedagogy into the backdrop of larger historical developments in Left politics and social movements. By understanding broader discourses within the politics of critical pedagogy, I believe that we are not only better able to point out the neglected areas within critical pedagogy, but also to begin to expand its horizon and redirect our focus. In doing so, we can better employ not only the strengths, but also address the shortcomings of critical pedagogy to forge new and alternative visions and politics of schooling.

I am a firm believer that schools and education can and should be an agent of change. Social change is what I am interested in, ultimately. I love the idea of education as a "change agent." But, I get frustrated when this word is overused and taken too easily among the "progressive" educators. Not long ago, I heard an ad for a university on the radio. The university was selling itself, claiming that it considers itself as an agent of change. Evidently, "education as a change agent" has now become a marketing slogan. Given that, I am not sure if we need to take this word more seriously, or to drop the idea entirely. The idea of schools as agents of change is not a monopoly of critical pedagogy. Critical pedagogy is not the only field to pursue and present education as an agency of social change. Since my ultimate interest continues to be in social change and education, I could have written this book, not focusing on critical pedagogy, but on critical education in general.

However, I decided to focus on critical pedagogy because I believed it to be an appropriate starting point for this book. From its beginning, critical pedagogy has proclaimed and identified itself as a search for the "language of possibility." In addition, critical pedagogy has been quite influential and popular within critical education theory. Therefore, critical pedagogy can be used as an effective litmus test to see whether or not, how far, and in what direction we have evolved and progressed in our search for alternative visions of education. Whether or not one identifies with critical pedagogy, and even if we had not invented a new field and named it "critical pedagogy," I think critical education would have gone beyond the "language of critique." The search for alternatives (the "language of possibility") was, indeed, a necessary next step for critical education to move forward.

Therefore, critical pedagogy has thrown the right and necessary question to critically minded educators: what are our alternatives? Isn't it time for critical educators to present alternative/counter-hegemonic visions of education? Of course, this is not a new question. For a long time, critically minded educators have been working on this very question: what are our alternatives? Yet, critical pedagogy has pushed us more forcefully to re-think and re-focus our energy for "alternatives." Due to the discourse field and theoretical trends at the time of its birth, critical pedagogy has ended up with a lopsided focus, as this book has shown. However, despite all its flaws, the question that critical pedagogy has raised remains the right one. It took a while, but I have come to realize that academia, too, has trends and fashions. Some theories and concepts become dominant and popular at one time, and then they are replaced by other theories and concepts, as fashion changes. Critical pedagogy has carried the question of alternative education for the last three decades. Globalization studies may take the baton, and carry the question farther. Or some other theories may come along and replace critical pedagogy. So, in the end, it does not seem to really matter what name one chooses to use, critical pedagogy, critical education, or whatever, as long as we do not forget the question of "what are our alternatives?" and continue to explore counter-hegemonic education.

REFERENCES

Adorno, T. (1938/1978). On the fetish-character in music and the regression of listening. In A. Arato & E. Gebhardt (Eds.), *The essential Frankfurt School reader* (pp. 270–299). New York: Urizen Books.

Adorno, T. (1962/1978). Commitment. In A. Arato & E. Gebhardt (Eds.), *The essential Frankfurt School reader* (pp. 300–318). New York: Urizen Books.

Adorno, T. (1973). *Negative dialectics*. New York: Seabury Press.

Ahmad, A. (1995). Postcolonialism: What's in a name? In R. Campa, E. Kaplan, & M. Sprinker (Eds.), *Late imperial culture* (pp. 11–32). New York: Verso.

Allen, R.L. (2004). Whiteness and critical pedagogy. *Educational Philosophy and Theory*, 36(2): 121–136.

Allman, P. (1999). *Revolutionary social transformation: Democratic hopes, political possibilities and critical education*. Westport, CT: Bergin & Garvey.

Allman, P. (2001). *Critical education against global capitalism*. Westport, CT: Bergin & Garvey.

Allman, P. (2007). *On Marx: An introduction to the revolutionary intellect of Karl Marx*. Rotterdam: Sense Publishers.

Althusser, L. (1971). *Lenin and philosophy and other essays*. B. Brewster (Trans.). New York: Monthly Review Press.

Amin, S. (1997). *Capitalism in the age of globalization*. New York: Zed Books.

Amin, S. (2004). *The liberal virus*. New York: Monthly Review Press.

Anyon, J. (2005). *Radical possibilities: Public policy, urban education, and a new social movement*. New York: Routledge.

Apple, M. (1979). *Ideology and curriculum*. New York: Routledge.

Apple, M. (1982). *Education and power*. Boston, MA: Routledge & Kegan Paul.

Apple, M. (2000). Can critical pedagogies interrupt rightist policies? *Educational Theory*, 50(2): 229–254.

Apple, M. (2001). *Educating the "right" way: Markets, standards, god, and inequality*. New York: RoutledgeFalmer.

Apple, M. (2010). *Global crises, social justice, and education: What can education do?* New York: Routledge.

Apple, M., Kenway, J., & Singh, M. (Eds.) (2005). *Globalizing education: Policies, pedagogies, & politics*. New York: Peter Lang.

Apple, M., & Buras, K. (Eds.) (2006). *The subaltern speak: Curriculum, power, and educational struggles*. New York: Routledge.

Arato, A. (1978). Introduction: Esthetic theory and cultural criticism. In A. Arato & E. Gebhardt (Eds.), *The essential Frankfurt School reader* (pp. 185–219). New York: Urizen Books.

Arato, A., & Gebhardt, E. (Eds.) (1978). *The essential Frankfurt School reader*. New York: Urizen Books.

Aronowitz, S. (1989). Working class identity and celluloid fantasies in the electronic age. In H. Giroux, R. Simon, & Contributors. *Popular culture: Schooling & everyday life* (pp. 197–217). Granby, MA: Bergin & Garvey.

Aronowitz, S., & Giroux, H. (1991). *Postmodern education: Politics, culture, & social criticism*. Minneapolis, MN: University of Minnesota Press.

Baudrillard, J. (1975). *The mirror of production*. St. Louis, MO: Telos Press.

Baudrillard, J. (1994). *Simulacra and simulation*. Ann Arbor, MI: University of Michigan Press.

Benjamin, W. (1937/1978). The author as producer. In A. Arato & E. Gebhardt (Eds.), *The essential Frankfurt School reader* (pp. 254–269). New York: Urizen Books.

Benton, T. (1993). *Natural relations: Ecology, animal rights and social justice*. London: Verso.

Bernal, D., Elenes, C.A., Goninez, F.E., & Villenas, S. (Eds.) (2006). *Chicana/Latina education in everyday life: Feminista perspectives on pedagogy and epistemology*. Albany, NY: State University of New York Press.

Biesta, G (1998). Say you want a revolution: Suggestions for the impossible future of critical pedagogy. *Educational Theory*, 48(4): 499–510.

Biesta, G. (2006). *Beyond learning: Democratic education for a human nature*. Boulder, CO: Paradigm.

Bourdieu, P. (1984). *Distinction: A social critique of the judgement of taste*. Cambridge, MA: Harvard University Press.

Bourdieu, P., & Passeron, J. (1977). *Reproduction in education, society and culture*. London: Sage.

Bourne, J. (1999). Racism, postmodernism and the flight from class. In D. Hill, P. Mclaren, M. Cole, & G. Rikowski (Eds.), *Postmodernism in educational theory: Education and the politics of human resistance* (pp. 131–146). London: The Tufnell Press.

Bowles, S., & Gintis, H. (1976). *Schooling in capitalist America: Educational reform and the contradictions of economic life*. New York: Basic Books.

Bowles, S., & Gintis, H. (2001). Schooling in Capitalist America revisited. Retrieved April 15, 2011, from www.umass.edu/preferen/gintis/soced.pdf.

Bratich, J., Packer, J., & McCarthy, C. (Eds.) (2003). *Foucault, cultural studies, and governmentality*. Albany, NY: State University of New York Press.

Brennan, T. (2006). *Wars of position: The cultural politics of Left and Right*. New York: Columbia University Press.

Burbules, N., & Torres, C. (2000). *Globalization and education: Critical perspectives*. New York: Routledge.

Buras, K., & Motter, P. (2006). Toward a subaltern cosmopolitan multiculturalism. In M. Apple & K. Buras (Eds.), *The subaltern speak: Curriculum, power, and educational struggles* (pp. 243–270). New York: Routledge.

Butler, J. (1997). Merely cultural. *Social Text*, 15(3/4): 264–277.

Carnoy, M., & Levin, H. (1985). *Schooling and work in the democratic state*. Stanford, CA: Stanford University Press.

Carnoy, M., & Rhoten, D. (2002). What does globalization mean for educational change? A comparative approach. *Comparative Education Review*, 46: 1–9.

Carroll-Miranda, J. (2011). Emancipatory technologies: A dialogue between hackers and Freire. In C. Malott & B. Porfilio (Eds.), *Critical pedagogy in the twenty-first century: A new generation of scholars* (pp. 521–539). Charlotte, NC: Information Age Publishing.

Castells, M. (1996). *The rise of the network society*. Boston, MA: Blackwell Publishers.

Castells, M., Flecha, R., Freire, P., Giroux, H., Macedo, D., & Willis, P. (1999). *Critical education in the new information age*. Lanham, MD: Rowman & Littlefield Publishers.

Césaire, A. (1955/2000). *Discourse on colonialism*. New York: Monthly Review Press.

Chan-Tiberghien, J. (2004). Towards a "global educational justice" research paradigm: Cognitive justice, decolonizing methodologies and critical pedagogy. *Globalization, Societies and Education*, 2(2): 191–213.

Connell, R.W. (1995). *Masculinities*. Berkeley, CA: University of California Press.

Counts, G.S. (1932). *Dare the school build a new social order?* New York: John Day Company.

Cote, M., Day, R., & Peuter, G. (Eds.) (2007). *Utopian pedagogy: Radical experiments against neoliberal globalization*. Toronto: University of Toronto Press.

Dale, R., Esland, G., Fergusson, R., & MacDonald, M. (Eds.) (1981). *Education and the state*. Barcombe, UK: Falmer Press.

Darder, A., Baltodano, M., & Torres, R. (Eds.) (2003). *The critical pedagogy reader*. New York: RoutledgeFalmer.

Darder, A., & Torres, R. (2004). *After race: Racism after multiculturalism*. New York: New York University Press.

Davis, M. (1999). *Prisoners of the American dream: Politics and economy in the history of the U.S. working class*. New York: Verso.

Delpit, L. (1995). *Other people's children: Cultural conflict in the classroom*. New York: New Press.

Denning, M. (2004). *Culture in the age of three worlds*. New York: Verso.

Dewey, J. (1902/1938). *Experience and education*. New York: Macmillan.

Du Bois, W.E.B. (1947/1975). *The world and Africa*. New York: International Publishers.

Duncan-Andrade. J., & Morrell, E. (2007). Critical pedagogy and popular culture in an urban secondary English classroom. In P. McLaren & J. Kincheloe (Eds.), *Critical pedagogy: Where are we now?* (pp. 183–199). New York: Peter Lang.

Duncan-Andrade, J., & Morrell, E. (2008). *Possibilities for moving from theory to practice in urban schools*. New York: Peter Lang.

D'Mello, B. (2009). What is Maoism? Retrieved January 6, 2012, from http://monthlyreview.org/commentary/what-is-maoism.

Eagleton, T. (1991). *Ideology: An introduction*. New York: Verso.

Ebert, T. (1996). *Ludic feminism: Postmodernism, desire, and labor in late capitalism*. Ann Arbor, MI: University of Michigan Press.

Elenes, C.A. (2003). Reclaiming the borderlands: Chicana/o identity, difference, and critical pedagogy. In A. Darder, M. Baltodano, & R. Torres (Eds.), *The critical pedagogy reader* (pp. 191–210). New York: RoutledgeFalmer.

Ellsworth, E. (1988/1992). Why doesn't this feel empowering? Working through the repressive myths of critical pedagogy. In C. Luke & J. Gore (Eds.), *Feminisms and critical pedagogy* (pp. 90–119). New York: Routledge.

Evans, P. (Ed.) (1996). *State-society synergy: Government and social capital in development*. International and Area Studies, University of California at Berkeley.

Fanon, F. (1963). *The wretched of the earth*. New York: Grove Press.

Fine, M. (2003). Sexuality, schooling, and adolescent females: The missing discourse of desire. In A. Darder, M. Baltodano, & R. Torres (Eds.), *The critical pedagogy reader* (pp. 296–321). New York: RoutledgeFalmer.

Fischman, G., Mclaren, P., Sünker, H., & Lankshear, C. (Eds.) (2005). *Critical theories, radical pedagogies, and global conflicts*. Lanham, MD: Rowman & Littlefield.

Foucault, M. (1977). *Discipline and punish: The birth of the prison*. New York: Vintage Books.

Foucault, M. (1980). *Power/knowledge: Selected interviews & other writings 1972–1977*. New York: Pantheon Books.

Foucault, M. (1988). *Technologies of the self: A seminar with Michael Foucault*. Amherst, MA: University of Massachusetts Press.

Foucault, M. (1999). *Religion and culture*. New York: Routledge.

Freire, P. (1970/1997). *Pedagogy of the oppressed*. M. Ramos (Trans.). New York: Continuum.

Gabbard, D. (2006). No "Coppertops" left behind: Foucault, the matrix, and the future of compulsory schooling. In A. Beaulieu & D. Gabbard (Eds.), *Michel Foucault and power today* (pp. 37–50). Lanham: Lexington Books.

George, S. (2004). *Another world is possible, if . . . .* New York: Verso.

Gilbert, A. (2011). Visions of hope and despair: Investigating the potential of critical science education. In C. Malott & B. Porfilio (Eds.), *Critical pedagogy in the twenty-first century: A new generation of scholars* (pp. 401–418). Charlotte, NC: Information Age Publishing.

Giroux, H. (1983). *Theory and resistance in education: A pedagogy for the opposition*. South Hadley, MA: Bergin & Garvey.

Giroux, H. (1988a). Border pedagogy in the age of postmodernism. *Journal of Education*, 170(2): 162–181.

Giroux, H. (1988b). *Teachers as intellectuals: Toward a critical pedagogy of learning*. South Hadley, MA: Bergin & Garvey.

Giroux, H. (Ed.) (1991). *Postmodernism, feminism, and cultural studies: Redrawing educational boundaries*. New York: State University of New York Press.

Giroux, H. (1992). *Border crossings: Cultural workers and the politics of education*. New York: Routledge.

Giroux, H. (1995). Insurgent multiculturalism and the promise of radical pedagogy. In D. Goldberg. (Ed.), *Multiculturalism: A critical reader* (pp. 325–343). Oxford: Blackwell.

Giroux, H. (1997). *Pedagogy and the politics of hope: Theory, culture, and schooling*. Boulder, CO: Westview Press.

Giroux, H. (2004). The terror of neoliberalism: Authoritarianism and the eclipse of democracy. Boulder, CO: Paradigm.

Giroux, H., & McLaren, P. (1989). *Critical pedagogy, the state, and cultural struggle*. Albany, NY: State University of New York Press.

Giroux, H., & McLaren, P. (1994). *Between borders: Pedagogy and the politics of cultural studies*. New York: Routledge.

Gitlin, T. (1980). *The whole world is watching: Mass media in the making and unmaking of the new left*. Berkeley, CA: University of California Press.

Gore, J. (1993). *The struggle for pedagogies: Critical and feminist discourses as regimes of truth*. New York: Routledge.

Gramsci, A. (1971). *Selections from the prison notebooks*. Q. Hoare & G.N. Smith (Eds. & Trans.). New York: International.

Grande, S. (2004). *Red pedagogy: Native American social and political thought*. Lanham, MD: Rowman & Littlefield Publishers.

Greene, M. (1967). *Existential encounters for teachers*. New York, Random House.

Greene, M. (1988). *The dialectic of freedom*. New York: Teachers College Press.

Greene, M. (1995). *Releasing the imagination: Essays on education, the arts, and social change*. San Francisco: Jossey-Bass Publishers.

Gruenewald, D., & Smith, G. (Eds.) (2007). *Place-based education in the global age: Local diversity*. New York: Lawrence Erlbaum Associates.

Gur-Ze'ev, I. (1998). Toward a nonrepressive critical pedagogy. *Educational Theory*, 48(4): 463–486.

Gur-Ze'ev, I. (2007). *Beyond the modern-postmodern struggle in education: Toward counter-education and enduring improvisation*. Rotterdam: Sense Publishers.

Habermas, J. (1975). *Legitimation crisis*. T. McCarthy (Trans.). Boston, MA: Beacon Press.

Habermas, J. (2001). *The postnational constellation: Political essays*. Cambridge, MA: MIT Press.

Hall, S. (1958). A sense of classlessness. *Universities and Left Review*, 1(5): 26–32.

Hall, S. (1980). Cultural studies: Two paradigms. *Media, Culture and Society*, 2(1): 57–72.

Hardt, M., & Negri, A. (2000). *Empire*. Cambridge, MA: Harvard University Press.

Harry, B., & Klingner, J. (2006). *Why are so many minority students in special education? Understanding race & disability in schools*. New York: Teachers College Press.

Harvey, D. (1990). *The condition of postmodernity*. Malden, MA: Blackwell.

Harvey, D. (2000). *Spaces of hope*. Berkeley, CA: University of California Press.

Harvey, D. (2003). *The new imperialism*. Oxford: Oxford University Press.

Harvey, D. (2010). Organizing for the anti-capitalist transition. *Brecht Forum, January 2010*. Retrieved April 15, 2011, from http://postcapitalist project.org/node/26.

Hearse, P. (Ed.) (2007). *Take the power to change the world: Globalisation and the debate on power*. London: Lighting Source.

Herbst, J. (2000). *States and power in Africa*. Princeton, NJ: Princeton University Press.

Hickman, H. (2011). Disrupting heteronormativity through critical pedagogy and queer theory. In C. Malott & B. Porfilio (Eds.), *Critical pedagogy in the twenty-first century: A new generation of scholars* (pp. 69–86). Charlotte, NC: Information Age Publishing.

Hindess, B., & Hirst, P. (1977). *Mode of production and social formation*. London: Macmillan.

Hirsch, E.D. (1988). *Cultural literacy: What every American needs to know*. New York: Vintage Books.

Hobsbawm, E. (1994). *The age of extremes: A history of the world, 1914–1991*. New York: Pantheon Book.

Hobsbawm, E. (2009). Socialism has failed. Now capitalism is bankrupt. So what comes next? *The Guardian*, April, 10, 2009. Retrieved April 15, 2011, from www.guardian.co.uk/commentisfree/2009/apr/10/financial-crisis-capitalism-socialism-alternatives.

Hoggart, R. (1957). *The use of literacy*. London: Penguin.

Holloway, J. (2002). *Change the world without taking power: The meaning of revolution today*. Ann Arbor, MI: Pluto Press.

hooks, b. (1984). *Feminist theory: From margin to center*. Boston, MA: South End Press.

hooks, b. (1994). *Teaching to transgress: Education as the practice of freedom*. New York: Routledge.

Jackson, P. (1968). *Life in classrooms.* New York: Holt, Rinehart and Winston.

Janesick, V. (2007). Reflections on the violence of high-stakes testing and the soothing nature of critical pedagogy. In P. McLaren & J. Kincheloe (Eds.), *Critical pedagogy: Where are we now?* (pp. 239–248). New York: Peter Lang.

Jay, M. (1973). *The dialectical imagination: A history of the Frankfurt School and the Institute of Social Research, 1923–1950.* Boston, MA: Little, Brown and Company.

Kahn, R. (2010). *Critical pedagogy, ecoliteracy, and planetary crisis.* New York: Peter Lang.

Karabel, J., & Halsey, A. (1977). Educational research: A review and an interpretation. In J. Karabel & A. Halsey (Eds.), *Power and ideology in education* (pp. 1–86). New York: Oxford University Press.

Kenny, L. (2000). *Daughters of suburbia: Growing up white, middle class, and female.* New Brunswick, NJ: Rutgers University Press.

Kincheloe, J. (2004). *Critical pedagogy primer.* New York: Peter Lang.

Kincheloe, J. (2007). Critical pedagogy in the twenty-first century: Evolution for survival. In P. McLaren & J. Kincheloe (Eds.), *Critical pedagogy: Where are we now?* (pp. 9–42). New York: Peter Lang.

Kincheloe, J., & Steinberg, S. (1998). Addressing the crisis of whiteness: Reconfiguring whiteness identity in a pedagogy of whiteness. In J. Kincheloe, S. Steinberg, N. Rodriguez, & R. Chennault (Eds.), *White reign: Deploying whiteness in America* (pp. 3–30). New York: St. Martin's Press.

Kress, T., & DeGennaro, D. (2011). Scaling the classroom walls: Lessons learned outside of schools about social media activism and education. In C. Malott & B. Porfilio (Eds.), *Critical pedagogy in the twenty-first century: A new generation of scholars* (pp. 473–495). Charlotte, NC: Information Age Publishing.

Laclau, E., & Mouffe, C. (1984). *Hegemony and socialist strategy.* New York: Routledge.

Ladson-Billings, G. (1994). *The dreamkeepers: Successful teachers of African American children.* San Francisco, CA: Jossey-Bass Publisher.

Lareau, A. (1989). *Home advantage: Social class and parental intervention in elementary education.* New York: Falmer Press.

Lather, P. (1991). *Getting smart: Feminist research and pedagogy with/in the postmodern.* New York: Routledge.

Lather, P. (1992). Post-critical pedagogies: A feminist reading. In C. Luke & J. Gore (Eds.), *Feminisms and critical pedagogy* (pp. 120–137). New York: Routledge.

Lather, P. (1998). Critical pedagogy and its complicities: A praxis of stuck places, *Educational Theory*, 48(4): 487–498.

Lechner, F., & Boli, J. (2005). *World culture: Origins and consequences.* Malden, MA: Blackwell.

Leite, J.C. (2005). *The World Social Forum: Strategies of resistance.* Chicago: Haymarket Books.

Leonardo, Z. (2002). The souls of white folk: Critical pedagogy, whiteness studies, and globalization discourse. *Race Ethnicity & Education*, 5(1): 29–50.

Leonardo, Z. (2003a). Resisting capital: Simulationist and socialist strategies. *Critical Sociology*, 29(2): 211–236.

Leonardo, Z. (2003b). Reality on trial: Notes on ideology, education, and utopia. *Policy Futures in Education*, 1(3): 504–525.

Leonardo, Z. (2004). The color of supremacy: Beyond the discourse of "white privilege". *Educational Philosophy and Theory*, 36(2): 137–152.

Leonardo, Z. (Ed.) (2005). *Critical pedagogy and race.* Malden, MA: Blackwell.

Leonardo, Z. (2006). Reality on trail: Notes on ideology, education, and utopia. In M. Peters & J. Freeman-Moir (Eds.), *Edutopias: New utopian thinking in education* (pp. 79–98). Rotterdam: Sense Publishers.

Leonardo, Z., & Porter, R. (2010). Pedagogy of fear: Toward Fanonian theory of "safety" in race dialogue. *Race, Ethnicity and Education*, 13: 139–157.

Lerner, M. (2006). *The Left hand of god: Taking back our country from the religious Right.* New York: HarperSanFrancisco.

Levine, D., Lowe, R., Peterson, R., & Tenorio, R. (Eds.) (1995) *Rethinking schools: An agenda for change.* New York: New Press.

Li, H. (2003). Bioregionalism and global action: A reexamination. *Educational Theory*, 53(1): 55–73.

Liou, D., & Antrop-González, R. (2011). To upend the boat of teacher mediocrity: The challenges and possibilities of critical race pedagogy in diverse urban classrooms. In C. Malott & B. Porfilio (Eds.), *Critical pedagogy in the twenty-first century: A new generation of scholars* (pp. 455–470). Charlotte, NC: Information Age Publishing.

Lissovoy, N. (2008). *Power, crisis, and education for liberation: Rethinking critical pedagogy.* New York: Palgrave Macmillan.

Loomba, A. (1998). *Colonialism/postcolonialism.* New York: Routledge.

Lukács, G. (1923/1971). *History and class consciousness.* Cambridge, MA: MIT Press.

Luke, C. (1992). Feminist politics in radical pedagogy. In C. Luke & J. Gore (Eds.), *Feminisms and critical pedagogy* (pp. 25–53). New York: Routledge.

Luke, C., & Gore, J. (Eds.) (1992). *Feminisms and critical pedagogy*. New York: Routledge.

Lund, D., & Carr, P. (Eds.) (2008). *Doing democracy: Striving for political literacy and social justice*. New York: Peter Lang.

Lynn, M. (2004). Inserting the "race" into critical pedagogy: An analysis of "race-based epistemologies". *Educational Philosophy and Theory*, 36(2): 153–166.

Lyotard, J. (1984). *The postmodern condition: A report on knowledge*. Minneapolis, MN: University of Minnesota Press.

Macdonald, A., & Sancher-Casal, S. (Eds.) (2002). *Twenty-first-century feminist classrooms: Pedagogies of identity and difference*. New York: Palgrave Macmillan.

MacLeod, J. (1995). *Ain't no makin' it: Aspirations and attainment in a low-income neighborhood*. Boulder, CO: Westview Press.

Mahler, F., & Tetreault, M. (Eds.) (2002). *The feminist classroom*. Lanham, MD: Roman & Littlefield.

Marcuse, H. (1969). *An essay on liberation*. Boston, MA: Beacon Press.

Marcuse, H. (1972). *Counterrevolution and revolt*. Boston, MA: Beacon Press.

Marshall, J. (1998). Michel Foucault: Philosophy, education, and freedom as an exercise upon the self. In M. Peters (Ed.), *Naming the multiple: Poststructuralism and education* (pp. 65–84). Westport, CO: Bergin & Garvey.

Martin, G., & Riele, K. (2011). A place-based critical pedagogy in turbulent times: Restoring hope for alternative futures. In C. Malott & B. Porfilio (Eds.), *Critical pedagogy in the twenty-first century: A new generation of scholars* (pp. 23–52). Charlotte, NC: Information Age Publishing.

McCarthy, C. (1998). *The uses of culture: Education and the limits of ethnic affiliation*. New York: Routledge.

McLaren, P. (1988). Schooling the postmodern body: Critical pedagogy and the politics of enfleshment. *Journal of Education*, 170(2): 53–83.

McLaren, P. (1989). *Life in schools: An introduction to critical pedagogy in the foundations of education*. New York: Longman.

McLaren, P. (1995). *Critical pedagogy and predatory culture*. New York: Routledge.

McLaren, P. (1997). *Revolutionary multiculturalism: Pedagogies of dissent for the new millennium*. Boulder, CO: Westview Press.

McLaren, P. (1998). Revolutionary pedagogy in post-revolutionary times: Rethinking the political economy of critical education. *Educational Theory*, 48(4): 431–462.

McLaren, P. (1999). Traumatizing capital: Oppositional pedagogies in the age of consent. In M. Castells, R. Flecha, P. Freire, H. Giroux, D. Macedo, & P. Willis (Eds.), *Critical education in the new information age* (pp. 1–36). Lanham, MD: Rowman & Littlefield Publishers.

McLaren, P. (2003). Critical pedagogy: A look at the major concepts. In A. Darder, M. Baltodano, & R. Torres (Eds.), *The critical pedagogy reader* (pp. 69–96). New York: RoutledgeFalmer.

McLaren, P. (2005). *Capitalism & conquerors: A critical pedagogy against empire*. Lanham, MD: Rowman & Littlefield.

McLaren, P., & Farahmandpur, R. (2001). Class, cultism, and multiculturalism: A notebook on forging a revolutionary politics. *Multicultural Education*, 8(3): 2–14.

McLaren, P., & Farahmandpur, R. (2005). *Teaching against global capitalism and the new imperialism: A critical pedagogy*. Lanham, MD: Rowman & Littlefield.

McLaren, P., & Jaramillo, N. (2007). *Pedagogy and praxis in the age of empire: Towards a new Humanism*. Rotterdam: Sense Publisher.

Mertes, T. (Ed.) (2004). *A movement of movements: Is another world really possible?* New York: Verso.

Mies, M. (1986). *Patriarchy and accumulation on a world scale*. New York: Zed Books.

Moore, R., & Muller, J. (1999). The discourse of "voice" and the problem of knowledge and identity in the sociology of education. *British Journal of Sociology of Education*, 20(2): 189–206.

Moraff, C. (2009). Ten years after Seattle: The global justice movement evolves. *In These Times, October 19, 2009*. Retrieved October 21, 2009, from www.inthesetimes.com/article/5027.

Morrow, R., & Torres, C. (2002). *Reading Freire and Habermas: Critical pedagogy and transformative social change*. New York: Teachers College Press.

Nanda, M. (1997). "History is what hurts": A materialist feminist perspective on the Green Revolution and its ecofeminist critics. In R. Hennessy & C. Ingraham (Eds.), *Materialist feminism: A reader in class, difference, and women's lives* (pp. 364–394). New York: Routledge.

Naples, N. (2003). *Feminism and method: Ethnography, discourse analysis, and activist research*. New York: Routledge.

Nash, G., Crabtree, C., & Dunn, R. (1997). *History on trial: Culture wars and the teaching of the past*. New York: Random House.

Noddings, N. (2005). *The challenge to care in schools: An alternative approach to education*. New York: Teachers College Press.

Olssen, M., & Peters, M. (2007). Marx, education, and the possibilities of a fairer world: Reviving radical political economy through Foucault. In A. Green, G. Rikowski, & H. Raduntz (Eds.), *Renewing dialogues in Marxism and education* (pp. 151–179). New York: Palgrave Macmillan.

Ong, A. (1987). *Spirits of resistance and capitalist discipline: Factory women in Malaysia*. Albany, NY: State University of New York Press.

Orelus, P. (2011). When theory walks with praxis: Critical pedagogy and the life of transnational and postcolonial subjects of color. In C. Malott & B. Porfilio (Eds.), *Critical pedagogy in the twenty-first century: A new generation of scholars* (pp. 3–21). Charlotte, NC: Information Age Publishing.

Orner, M. (1992). Interrupting the calls for student voice in "liberatory" education: A feminist poststructuralist perspective. In C. Luke & J. Gore (Eds.), *Feminisms and critical pedagogy* (pp. 74–89). New York: Routledge.

Paik, S., & Walberg, H. (Eds.) (2007). *Narrowing the achievement gap: Strategies for educating Latino, Black and Asian students*. New York: Springer.

Palermo, J. (2002). *Poststructuralist readings of the pedagogical encounter*. New York: Peter Lang.

Parker, L., & Stovale, D. (2004). Actions following words: Critical race theory connects to critical pedagogy. *Educational Philosophy and Theory*, 36(2): 167–182.

Peters, M., & Roberts, P. (2000). Universities, futurology and education. *Discourse*, 21(2): 125–139.

Peters, M., & Freeman-Moir, J. (2006). *Edutopias: New utopian thinking in education*. Rotterdam: Sense Publishers.

Peters, M., & Besley, T. (2007). *Subjectivity and truth: Foucault, education, and the culture of self*. New York: Peter Lang.

Petras, J. (1997). Imperialism and NGOs in Latin America. *Monthly Review*, 49(7): 10–33.

Petras, J., & Veltmeyer, H. (2005). *Social movements and state power: Argentina, Brazil, Olivia, Ecuador*. Ann Arbor, MI: Pluto Press.

Piccone, P. (1978). General introduction. In A. Arato & E. Gebhardt (Eds.), *The essential Frankfurt School reader* (pp. xi–xxiii). New York: Urizen Books.

Pinar, W. (2010). Foreword. In J. Sandlin, B. Schulyz, & J. Burdick (Eds.), *Handbook of public pedagogy: Education and learning beyond schooling* (pp. xv–xix). New York: Routledge.

Pollock, F. (1941/1978). State capitalism: Its possibilities and limitations. In A. Arato & E. Gebhardt (Eds.), *The essential Frankfurt School reader* (pp. 71–94). New York: Urizen Books.

Popkewitz, T., & Brennan, M. (1997). *Foucault's challenge: Discourse, knowledge, and power in education.* New York: Teachers College Press.

Popkewitz, T., & Fendler, L. (Eds.) (1999). *Critical theories in education: Changing terrains of knowledge and politics.* New York: Routledge.

Posner, G. (2004). *Analyzing the curriculum.* Boston, MA: McGraw-Hill.

Putnam, R. (1993). *Making democracy work: Civic traditions in modern Italy.* Princeton, NJ: Princeton University Press.

Reay, D. (1998). *Class work: Mothers' involvement in their children's primary schooling.* New York: Routledge.

Reid, A. (2005). Rethinking the democratic purposes of public schooling in a globalizing world. In M. Apple, J. Kenway, & M. Singh (Eds.), *Globalizing education: Policies, pedagogies, & politics* (pp. 281–296). New York: Peter Lang.

Ropers-Huilman, B. (1998). *Feminist teaching in theory and practice: Situating power and knowledge in poststructural classrooms.* New York: Teachers College Press.

Sader, E. (2004). Beyond civil society. In T. Mertes (Ed.), *A movement of movements: Is another world really possible?* (pp. 248–261). New York: Verso.

Sanbonmatsu, J. (2004). *The postmodern prince.* New York: Monthly Review Press.

Sandlin, J., Schulyz, B., & Burdick, J. (Eds.) (2010). *Handbook of public pedagogy: Education and learning beyond schooling.* New York: Routledge.

Santos, S.S.B. (2006). *The rise of the global Left: The World Social Forum and beyond.* New York: Zed Books.

Saul, J. (2005). *The next liberation struggle: Capitalism, socialism and democracy in southern Africa.* New York: Monthly Review Press.

Scatamburlo-D'Annibale, V., & McLaren, P. (2004). Class dismissed? Historical materialism and the politics of difference. *Educational Philosophy and Theory,* 36(2): 183–199.

Scott, J. (1992). Experience. In J. Butler & J. Scott (Eds.), *Feminists theorize the political* (pp. 22–40). New York: Routledge.

Shaker, P., & Heilman, E. (2008). *Reclaiming education for democracy: Thinking beyond No Child Left Behind.* New York: Routledge.

Shilling, C. (1992). Reconceptualising structure and agency in the sociology of education: Structuration theory and schooling. *British Journal of Sociology of Education*, 13(1): 69–87.

Shiva, V. (2005). *Earth democracy*. Cambridge, MA: South End Press.

Shor, I. (1992). *Empowering education: Critical teaching for social change*. Chicago, IL: The University of Chicago Press.

Sidorkin, A. (1997). Carnival and domination: Pedagogies of neither care nor justice. *Educational Theory*, 47(2): 229–238.

Singh, M., Kenway, J., & Apple, M. (2005). Globalizing education: Perspectives from above and below. In M. Apple, J. Kenway, & M. Singh (Eds.), *Globalizing education: Policies, pedagogies, & politics* (pp. 1–29). New York: Peter Lang.

Sloterdijk, P. (1997). *Critique of cynical reason*. M. Eldred (Trans.). Minneapolis, MN: University of Minnesota Press.

Smith, M. (2000). *Culture: Reinventing the social sciences*. Philadelphia, PA: Open University Press.

Sparks, C. (1996). Stuart Hall, cultural studies and Marxism. In D. Morley & K. Chen (Eds.), *Stuart Hall: Critical dialogues in cultural studies* (pp. 71–101). New York: Routledge.

Spring, J. (1989). *The sorting machine revisited: National educational policy since 1945*. New York: Longman.

Spring, J. (2007). *A new paradigm for global school systems: Education for a long and life*. Mahwah, NJ: Lawrence Erlbaum.

Spring, J. (2008a). *The intersection of cultures: Multicultural education in the United States and the global economy*. New York: Lawrence Erlbaum.

Spring, J. (2008b). Research on globalization and education. *Review of Educational Research*, 78(2): 330–363.

St. Pierre, E., & Pillow, W. (2000). *Working the ruins: Feminist poststructural theory and methods in education*. New York: Routledge.

Stromquist, N., & Monkman, K. (Eds.) (2000). *Globalization and education: Integration and contestation across cultures*. Lanham, MD: Rowman & Littlefield.

Suoranta, J., & Vadén, T. (2007). From social to socialist media: The critical potential of the Wikiworld. In P. McLaren & J. Kincheloe (Eds.), *Critical pedagogy: Where are we now?* (pp. 143–162). New York: Peter Lang.

Szwed, J. (1997). *Space is the place: The lives and times of Sun Ra*. New York: Pantheon Books.

Tang, E. (2005). The non-profit & the autonomous grassroots. *Left Turn Magazine*, 18, November 1, 2005. Retrieved April 15, 2011, from http://postcapitalistproject.org/node/56.

Teodori, M. (Ed.) (1969). *The New Left: A documentary history*. Indianapolis, IN: Bobbs-Merrill.

Thompson, E.P. (1957). Socialism and the intellectuals. *Universities and Left Review*, 1(1): 31–36.

Thompson, E.P. (1958). Agency and choice: A reply to criticism. *New Reasoner*, Summer: 88–106.

Tikly, L. (2001). Globalisation and education in the postcolonial world: Towards a conceptual framework. *Comparative Education*, 37(2): 151–171.

Tilly, C. (2004). *Social movements, 1768–2004*. Boulder, CO: Paradigm Publishers.

Touraine, A. (1971). *The May movement: Revolt and reform*. New York: Random House.

Trifonas, P. (Ed.) (2003). *Pedagogies of difference: Rethinking education for social change*. New York: RoutledgeFalmer.

Villegas, M., Neugebauer, S., & Venegas, K. (Eds.) (2008). *Indigenous knowledge and education: Sites of struggle, strength, and survivance*. Cambridge, MA: Harvard Educational Review.

Vygotsky, L. (1978). *Mind in society: The development of higher psychological processes*. Cambridge, MA: Harvard University Press.

Vygotsky, L. (1997). *Educational psychology*. Boca Raton, FL: St. Lucie Press.

Wallerstein, I. (1995). *After liberalism*. New York: The New Press.

Wallerstein, I. (2004a). *World-Systems analysis: An introduction*. Durham, NC: Duke University Press.

Wallerstein, I. (2004b). New revolts against the system. In T. Mertes (Ed.), *A movement of movements: Is another world really possible?* (pp. 262–273). New York: Verso.

Wallerstein, I. (2006). *European universalism: The rhetoric of power*. New York: The New Press.

Watkins, W. (Ed.) (2005). *Black protest thought and education*. New York: Peter Lang.

Weiler, K., & Mitchell, C. (Eds.) (1992). *What schools can do: Critical pedagogy and practice*. Albany, NY: State University of New York Press.

Weis, L. (1990). *Working class without work: High school students in a de-industrializing economy*. New York: Routledge.

Williams, R. (1961). *The long revolution*. London: Chatto & Windus.

Williams, R. (1963). *Culture and society, 1780–1950*. London: Penguin.

Willis, P. (1977). *Learning to labor: How working class kids get working class jobs*. New York: Columbia University Press.

Wrigley, T. (2006). *Another school is possible*. London: Bookmarks Publications & Trentham Books.

Young, M. (Ed.) (1971). *Knowledge and control: New directions for the sociology of education*. London: Collier Macmillan.

Young, M. (2000). Rescuing the sociology of educational knowledge from the extremes of voice discourse: Towards a new theoretical basis for the sociology of curriculum. *British Journal of Sociology of Education*, 21(4): 523–536.

Zavarzadeh, M., & Morton, D. (1994). *Theory as resistance: Politics and culture after (post)structuralism*. New York: Guilford Press.

Zinn, H. (1980). *A people's history of the United States*. New York: Harper & Row.

INDEX